Business Notes

Writing Personal Notes
That Build
Professional Relationships

Florence Isaacs

Clarkson N. Potter/Publishers
New York

To Harvey

Published by Clarkson N. Potter, Inc., 201 East 50th Street, New York, New York 10022. Member of the Crown Publishing Group.

Random House, Inc. New York, Toronto, London, Sydney, Auckland
www.randomhouse.com

CLARKSON N. POTTER, POTTER, and colophon are trademarks of Random House, Inc.

Printed in the United States of America

Library of Congress Cataloging-in-Publication Data
Isaacs, Florence.
Business notes : writing personal notes that build professional
relationships / by Florence Isaacs.
1. Business communication.   I. Title.
HF5718.I8   1998
657.7′4—dc21   97-27152

ISBN 0-517-70891-4

10

Contents

— ● —

Preface

This is a low-tech book for a high-tech world. It's about common sense, connecting with people, and ideas that cost nothing except a few minutes of your time, yet pay important dividends for your business and career. At a time when it's hard to get a live person on the telephone and the world operates on voice mail, a personal note is a powerful tool. People appreciate it and respond to it in a way they don't to other means of communication.

When I began this project, a few skeptics couldn't understand how writing a note could make any impact in the fast-paced business world. Their common lament was, "Who has the time for such projects?" Yet the majority of people I talked to were eager to share their own positive experiences or to discuss a genuine desire to communicate more effectively. For many of them, however, the fear of writing was as strong as the interest in writing.

Writing a book is an adventure. You never know what kind of information you will discover. In the process of exploring innovative applications for notes, I interviewed a range of professionals, and I found some surprises. One early revelation was that the more impressive the job titles, the more successful the rainmakers, the more likely they were to appreciate and use personal notes to woo new clients, cultivate customer loyalty, and motivate employees. Notes helped forge and maintain a web of relationships in and outside of their companies. Is there a link between notes and their success? They think so. The business leaders of today's world got where they are by making connections, and that's what writing notes is really about.

— • —

Though I cannot name all who have contributed to this book, I must acknowledge some for assistance that enriched the entire project. I met Fred Linch, owner of the Linch Company, at the first signing for my previous book, *Just a Note to Say . . . The Perfect Words for Every Occasion.* His imaginative use of business notes convinced me I was on the right track. Jon Prince, vice president of the McKeesport Candy Company, another dedicated note writer, also provided valuable help. I got extraordinary support from my editor, Pam Krauss.

For their insights, I also thank Samuel S. Perelson; Steven D. Oppenheim; Neil P. Lewis; Barbara Pachter of Pachter and Associates; S. B. Hirni of Echo Marketing Consultants; Dorothea Johnson, director of the Protocol School of Washington; Eileen Castolene, vice president, career transition, at Drake Beam Morin; Gayle Kosterman, senior vice president, human resources, at S. C. Johnson & Son; Gerald Sherwin, senior partner in charge of account service at Bozell Worldwide; James W. Viera, senior vice president of Cosmair; Gerry McLaughlin, senior vice president and associate creative director of Cline, Davis & Mann; Nancy R. Olsen, editor of *Pen World* magazine; Eve Cohen, president of the Aster Search Group; Geoffrey Berliner of Berliner Pen; Linda K. Shah; Dempsey & Carroll; Joan DeMayo; and Judith C. Tingley.

Part One

The Basics

The Value of Notes

Every Monday morning a senior partner in a large accounting firm leaves his home at 7:00 A.M. for the office. Tucked into his bulging briefcase is a fistful of clippings from the weekend newspapers: an ad for a business opportunity of interest to a client, an article on a tax issue recently discussed with a colleague, a notice of a friend's promotion, an engagement announcement for the child of someone who refers business to the accounting firm. When the partner arrives at the office, his first task of the day is to write a personal note to mail out with each clip.

Writing notes has become part of his work routine. Why does he bother? Because he understands that the world has changed. "Years ago, people established deep, stable business and professional relationships," he explains. "Loyalty really meant something. But today it's out of sight, out of mind. Anything you can do to remind people you're alive and available, without being too obvious about it, is valuable. A note is something tangible that keeps your name in front of present clients and those you're courting."

The CEO of a small company explains why *he*

writes notes as part of his regular routine: "Building relationships with customers and being thoughtful about their needs is a major part of what business is all about. It's no more sophisticated than that. When you write, 'Thank you for your business,' you let people know that you care about them. Then what do they do? They talk about you. If they see someone who needs your product or service, they say, 'Go see this guy.' We're all very attracted to courtesy because we get so little of it today."

In this age of global competition and technology, where everything changes fast, the personal touch is so rare that it stands out. It gets remembered. "Personal notes help distinguish me from the rest of the pack," says a management consultant, "and clients appreciate the effort. It makes a difference."

Personal notes are your own marketing and sales tools. They can build relationships, raise your visibility, and give you an extra edge. They're a smart business practice in a fast-paced world, and they get read precisely because they *are* notes. "People don't want to write a lot of stuff," says the executive vice president of a commercial bank, "and they don't want to read a lot, either. If I get a two-page letter, I say, 'I'll read it later.' Then maybe I don't look at it for a day or two. But I read a note right away."

The word "note," incidentally, generally refers to informal, brief correspondence in this book. Though a note may be written on letterhead in certain situations, it conveys a personal quality. It may be written by hand.

Reaching Those Who Count

There are many ways to use notes. They connect you not only to customers or clients but also to others who can do you some good. A note can act as a powerful follow-up to a meeting, an event, or a sales call; it can build goodwill and encourage repeat orders. Notes are also a way to stay in touch with people who refer business to you. They show that you're interested in something more than the next sale or what someone can do for you.

Notes can also motivate employees and help strengthen relationships with colleagues and others who may affect your performance. They're ideal networking tools at a time when you can't know too many people. Contacts in your field are sources of trade information who can save you enormous amounts of time and trouble. Notes are one way to maintain these crucial connections.

Contacts can also provide job leads. Says a psychologist who advises corporations, "Your network is your Rolodex. If you wait till you're laid off to start networking, it's probably too late. You need to connect with people at professional meetings and industry events—to see, be seen, and interact." And then follow up—with a note.

When you're actively job-hunting, notes can open doors. A good, brief cover letter can call attention to your résumé and help move it to the top of the pile. A thank-you note after an interview can reinforce the positive impression you made, and it may even get you the job.

During the process of hiring a vice president of manufacturing, one major corporation narrowed the field down to three people. A consultant who was called in to assess the candidates recalls: "The two strongest were neck and neck when we had all three back for a final interview. After the interviews, one wrote thank-you notes to me, the vice president of human resources, and the president of the company. Until then, it was a dead heat, and I can honestly say the notes tipped the scales. We felt that the candidate who wrote was warmer and had more compassion, and the notes were prime examples of those qualities."

Relationships with vendors and service providers, partners in joint ventures, government officials, and others you deal with or need help from, time and time again can also make or break your business life. It costs nothing to write a few words to a supplier: "Thank you. You did a good job." It's worth doing because the next time you need something, the supplier will remember your thanks and take good care of you. A note can also be a means of introducing yourself to someone you're trying to reach. Many television anchorpersons write personal notes to woo potential interviewees.

Notes can help strengthen bonds with competitors and opponents as well. Cordial relationships with your rivals will help you build a good reputation. Word gets around, and a warm rapport can help smooth the way if you face one another.

Notes build bridges internally, too—with your superiors, your subordinates, and your peers. They're a way to connect with people who can support you politically and help you get your work done. Notes of appreciation are tools to build loyalty and hold on to valued people. The pat-on-the-back note you sent to your secretary last month makes it likelier that she will work late tonight to get out that rush presentation.

Business-Related Social Occasions

The lines between business and social interactions often blur or overlap. Job-related friendships can last long after you or your friend moves on to another company or venture.

"After you've worked with people for a long time, you tend to get invited to all sorts of things. Work has been a significant source of personal friends for my family and me," says one computer industry executive.

Who hasn't been invited to the wedding of a colleague, marked a milestone birthday of a customer, or celebrated the birth of an associate's child? Notes are a way to acknowledge that people have lives outside of work—families, hopes, and dreams—and to recognize the events that are important to everyone. A personal note, with or without a gift, affirms the bonds you share and expresses friendship. It also reflects good manners and graciousness.

It may be necessary to write at other, less joyous, occasions. A get-well or condolence note says, "You matter to me as a human being, not only within the confines of the business world."

A New Way of Thinking

On the most basic level, notes can keep your name up front, speak eloquently about you and your company, and create a sense of community with those who affect your work, your bottom line, your life. They can sometimes even change an outcome in your favor or deliver an order. The business world is a tough one, but we're all human, and we respond when we feel a personal connection.

Says a business owner who writes notes all the time, "I'm in a very competitive business, and I need to ask myself what I can offer people that they can't get elsewhere. What makes my company different from other companies? The answer is this: I treat others as I want to be treated. Anytime you take the trouble to make people feel they're special, they put a marker down and act accordingly. A note does that, because it shows you took the time and you care."

A note also makes an impact because it's something tangible—something that you can touch and feel. It has a presence and a permanence. Says the owner mentioned above, "You send an E-mail to somebody, and in about thirty seconds the person receives it, reads it, and it's gone. When was the last time you saved an E-mail message or a fax?"

Yet people often crow about notes they've received and show them around to others. They might post them on company bulletin boards. The exposure can be multiplied many times.

What's missing in E-mail is the warmth of human contact and the expressive quality conveyed on a piece of paper—sometimes typed, sometimes handwritten, but always signed by you. As we get busier and technology takes over, the challenge is to preserve the personal element. Notes slow us down and say, "*This* is important. *You* are important."

There's also a bonus for the writer—the satisfaction and pleasure of thoughtful expression. It reminds us of an age when pulses didn't race quite so fast, when there was time to enjoy our lives and connect as people.

Opportunities are all around you to use notes, regardless of the field you're in or the position you hold. How can you write effective notes? "It's so hard to say something that isn't the same old same old, to make it interesting, not boring," laments one transportation industry executive. Yes, it is, unless you know how. There's really nothing mysterious about it. The fact is, if you can talk, you can compose a good note. Whether you write one that stands alone or add a few personal lines to a business letter or a printed card, you can produce notes that work for you and that will be appreciated.

To master the art of note-writing, all you have to do is follow some simple guidelines that are guaranteed to help you succeed every time—even if writing has always intimidated you. It does take some effort, but successful note writers *expect* to make an effort and view it as an investment. They take the time because notes pay off. "If you're just a little bit better these days, people remember you," says the CEO of an office equipment company. If you make note-writing a habit, they'll remember you, too.

2

What's in a Note?

A former colleague wins an award. A client opens a new office. A contact provides a lead on a job opening. A customer hasn't reordered in months. Situations like these arise all the time, and each is an opportunity to use a personal note to strengthen a business relationship.

The whole point of a note is brevity and clarity. But a good note must also say something. The message is specific to the person you're addressing and to his or her situation. That's what makes it personal and powerful—and why you shouldn't simply copy a model exactly. What you write will be different from what someone else writes because your voice and personality are unique, as are the individual relationships and situations that inspire your note-writing.

The guidelines that follow will help you find your focus and write smarter, more effective notes than you ever thought possible. Try them—you'll be amazed at the results.

Target the recipient. A successful note says, "I am talking to *you*." To convey that message, ask yourself,

"Who is this person and what is his or her position relative to me?" Are you addressing your boss, an employee, or a co-worker? Are you talking to a customer, a supplier, or a friendly competitor? These factors will certainly affect the language and maybe even the stationery you use; they will also make an impact on the substance and tone of your message. A note congratulating a client on a big contract will sound different from one to a colleague who has been promoted.

Ask yourself how well you know the person. Are you writing to someone you met last night at a banquet or to a person you've dealt with for years? Do the two of you talk every day, every week, once a year? Have you developed a personal relationship? How close is it? Do you chat about spouses and kids and football scores? Do you socialize outside of work? Your answers will help determine how formal or casual you want your writing style to be. For example, you'll write a more personal condolence or retirement note, and you'll have more to write *about,* when you're addressing a close friend than you would when writing to a casual acquaintance.

Consider your purpose. Why are you writing? What do you want to achieve? Do you want to motivate, inform, sell, or remind, or are you simply fulfilling an obligation? Your goals will shape the style and content of your note. A "thank you for the referral" note, for instance, is not only a courtesy but also a way to reinforce your relationship with someone who has sent new business your way. In a cover letter for a résumé, your aim is to get noticed fast.

Examine your own feelings. Your feelings *do* count, whether or not you decide to express them, and they can make a note sound genuine and sincere. Do you like and respect this person? If so, you can reflect these feelings in a "congratulations on your promotion" note. Will you miss someone who is leaving the company? Why not tell the person? Do you value a particular client? Say so by adding a handwritten note to a Christmas or New Year's card: "Your business means a great deal to us." Sharing your feelings makes a note personal and special.

Focus the message. The main issue is this: What do you want to say? Is it "Thanks for listening to my presentation. I hope you'll choose my company"? Or "I'm sorry you got downsized"? You may not use those exact words, but once you know what you want to express, you can begin to write a strong, clear message.

Devices You Can Use

We all can use extra help, especially when we feel stymied and stuck. Here are some techniques that will help uncork the flow of words and add impact to your notes. To take advantage of them, it's important to stretch your powers of observation, to notice things you may not have been alert to before, and to make connections. Careful listening is crucial as well. People will tell you a lot about themselves if you let *them* do the talking while you pay close attention.

Make your message specific. If you're going to take the trouble to write, say something specific to the person to increase your impact. Instead of saying, "Thank you for your help," spell it out, as in "Thank you for helping us at the new plant site. All our distributors thought it was wonderful."

Try to mention a specific topic you discussed or a special connection you share. One way you can do that is by recalling an earlier conversation. In a note following up a meeting, for example, you might comment on something the two of you talked about, whether or not it had to do with business, as in "Here's the information we discussed yesterday. Hope your flight to Houston wasn't delayed after all," or "Here's the list of restaurants we enjoyed in London. Hope you and David have a great vacation." Refer to interests you share, like baseball. If you used to work together, you can mention meeting someone both of you knew on the job, as in, "By the way, I bumped into Fred Patterson at lunch yesterday. He sends his regards."

People appreciate knowing that you paid attention to their concerns, and the logical response is "This is someone thoughtful—someone I'd feel comfortable doing business with." A specific reference communicates, "I know who *you* are," and it also jogs the person's memory and says, "Remember who *I* am." As you meet someone, start thinking about details you can mention later. When one marketing consultant exchanges business cards at industry events, he jots notes about the person on the back of each card: "just had twins" or "interested in pension plans." Then, when he comes across a helpful brochure on pension plans, he can send it with a note saying, "This might address some of the concerns you mentioned. Enjoyed meeting you at the trade show." He might also add, "Hope the twins are doing well."

Mention the person's hobbies or interests. What do you know about the person that can be useful when you write? What can you talk about besides your product or service? Is the person a marathon runner, a tennis player, a koi fancier, or a gourmet cook? Is he or she interested in travel, music, or gardening? Refer to the person's interests when you write, as in "The conference is set for July 16. See you there. P.S. Good luck with your tomato crop."

How do you glean information like this when you know someone only on a strictly professional basis? The single best thing you can do is look around the person's office or conference room. The walls and bookshelves will tell you volumes, even if you've just met for the first time.

Do you see books on photography or novels by Charles Dickens, contemporary art or a plaque for service to charity? Is there a humidor on the desk, a cactus plant on the floor, or a telescope at the window? How about golf or fishing memorabilia? Any of these objects will give you something talk about, even if it's not an interest you share.

Send clippings. "Just to write 'I enjoyed meeting you this afternoon' is a waste of time," says an advertising executive. "I drop those notes into the garbage can. You have to say something—that there's a meeting scheduled, or 'You mentioned you like red wine, and I just came across this article on the best reds.' It's flattering to get a note like that. Obviously someone thought enough about what you said, what you were interested in, to take the time to write."

Many businesses announce promotions in professional and trade publications. "I always tear these out and scrawl a personal message like 'I know you'll be running the place soon.' It's easier and less formal than writing a whole letter," says a publishing executive.

One professional finds newspaper announcements of weddings extraordinarily useful. "When I see one for somebody I know, I clip it and send it with a note saying, 'Congratulations. Thought you might like an extra copy for your scrapbook.' *Everybody* wants an extra copy," he says. And many people call to say thank you, which invariably leads to an opportunity to talk business. Sometimes the announcement includes interesting information about the person that you can mention in your note—for instance, "I didn't know you were on the school board."

Use quotes and statistics. A quote can often express a thought more eloquently than you could yourself, and it can serve as an introduction to what you have to say. Quotations are ideal for New Year's messages because we tend to get philosophical at that time. Be sure, however, to choose one that fits the occasion, pertains to the person, and reflects you as well.

This might work for a colleague's birthday: "We don't grow older, we grow riper"—Pablo Picasso.

For someone who is changing fields, how about this quotation: "Follow your bliss and don't be afraid. Doors will open where you didn't know they were going to be"—Joseph Campbell.

This might fit for someone who is quitting a job to start his or her own business: "Fortune favors the bold"—Juvenal.

For a friend who's debating whether or not to take a job offer, how about this: "He who hesitates is last"—Mae West.

Statistics relevant to someone's business or personal life come in handy, too: "I just read that exports are down 10 percent. Perhaps now is a good time to evaluate your program. I have some ideas that might interest you. How about lunch?"

You can find suitable quotes in a variety of books of quotations available in libraries and bookstores. A few titles are listed in the Reference Library at the back of this book. Good sources of statistics include the *Wall Street Journal*, the *New York Times, USA Today,* trade publications, and the Internet.

Consider all-purpose lines. Sometimes it's less important to be original than simply to be *heard.* On such occasions as a birth or a wedding, it's perfectly acceptable to write a heartfelt, if familiar, sentiment such as "It's great to hear that Jason Junior has arrived," or "I wish you two the very best of everything."

"I'm thinking of you" says a whole lot in a condolence note or a get-well message. The word "how," as in "How thoughtful" or "How generous," adds enthusiasm to a thank-you note. Or try beginning with the word "what," as in "What a great job you did on the brief" or "What great news" or "What a useful gift." This works well on any number of occasions.

Finding the Words

The best notes are concise and to the point. And you may be surprised to learn that it's often more difficult to write a short note than a long-winded letter. Just because the note itself is short doesn't mean you won't spend a little time writing it.

"The worst thing you can do is just dash something off without any thought," says a tax attorney. "That implies how little importance you place on the person —that you don't care enough to do it right. I regard language as a precise tool but one that requires constant sharpening. It takes me fifteen minutes to write a two-sentence condolence note to someone at the office. I firmly believe you should apply the same rules of refinement to your business life as you do to your personal life."

How do you proceed? Step number one is to slow yourself down and relax enough to stretch your creative muscles. Give yourself permission to let your mind wander and allow your thoughts to flow freely, without mental editing. Censor thoughts like "That's ridiculous" or "I can't say *that*." You don't want to quash ideas and feelings before you even experience them. Writing is full of surprises and self-censorship at this early stage can shut down the creative flow. Take out some scrap paper and put the words down without judgment of any kind. Worry about spelling and grammar later, *after* you know what you want to say. Some powerful words are likely to tumble out.

— • —

Here are some more tips to help you craft a good note:

Write conversationally. Everyone is afraid of making mistakes, but the secret is to write as simply and clearly as you can—the same way you'd talk in face-to-face conversation. If you wouldn't *say* it, don't write it. You wouldn't say "amongst" or "upon" or "in receipt of" or "please be advised." You wouldn't say "at the earliest opportunity" or "contained herein." These words are not businesslike; they're stuffy and boring. Skip the obscure ten-syllable words, too. This is not a vocabulary test; it's *communication*. If it's easy to read, it will get read. Consider a note written by an executive to a close colleague: "This project was on life support until you stepped in and turned it around. Thanks for a great job." That note sounds genuine and real.

To loosen up, talk into a tape recorder. When you hear your own words you'll be amazed at how natural and well-chosen they sound.

Beware of humor. What's funny to you may not amuse someone else. On the other hand, a light touch, handled well, is usually welcome. Did a friend receive a long sought-after promotion? "Hallelujah! You finally got it," might bring a smile. The safest course is to know the person you're talking to and use your judgment. Play it straight in international correspondence, however. Humor is a thicket when you cross cultural lines, say experts.

Avoid using jargon. It's your job to know your audience. For instance, if you're an engineer, unless you're talking to *another* engineer who speaks the same language, beware of causing communication problems by using industry slang. Will your client understand what you mean when you mention section 1024 of the tax code? If not, explain it. Some people hide behind mysterious terminology, believing it makes them look knowledgeable. But complicated language is not profound; it's frustrating, unreadable, and annoying.

Keep your notes correct and neat. Errors in grammar and spelling say a lot about you—none of it good. Neatness counts, too—no coffee stains or cross-outs allowed. One professional who was looking for a job sent a résumé to a networking contact who had offered to pass it along to a third party. Says the contact, "I was shocked. It was full of typos, and the paper was all crumpled. I had to call and say, 'This is inappropriate.' I will not recommend this person again."

Keep a thesaurus on your desk, as professional writers do, and refer to it regularly to vary your language, choosing only words whose use is familiar to you. The same words used over and over again deaden your prose. Use precise, active verbs, too. Look at the contrast between "The seminar was educational" and "The seminar energized everyone." But always choose words that suit your voice; if you pick fussy or unfamiliar words out of a book, they'll be out of place in your note.

Tone

Business correspondence has become more casual in recent years, but you need to decide just *how* informal you want to sound. Your tone will depend on the purpose of the note, your relationship with the recipient, the age and openness of the person, and the corporate culture. An announcement to the entire organization will usually sound more formal than a note of congratulations to an individual. When in doubt, it's better to err on the side of formality rather than take a chance on sounding too familiar.

When you do want to establish a casual tone, contractions can help, as in "Here's" rather than "Here is." "Thanks" is less formal than "thank you." It's also less formal if you eliminate a pronoun, as in "Enjoyed meeting you," rather than "I enjoyed meeting you."

Begin your note with "Dear Mr. So-and-So" or "Dear Ms. Jones" unless you're already on a solid first-name basis. Write more formally in international correspondence than you might here in the United States, and use the full name if you don't know the sex of the person. "When the name of someone you haven't met is something like Pat Smith," says an etiquette expert, "just write, 'Dear Pat Smith.' You don't want to guess 'Mr.' and then discover it's wrong."

Close with "Sincerely" or "Sincerely yours" or "Cordially." If you're using a less formal tone, you might sign off with "Best" or "Regards." " 'Best regards' says 'I'd love to do business with you,' " says a banker. He also likes "Warm regards." "Warmly" can work if you know the person well, but avoid "Affectionately" in any business circumstance.

Handwritten versus Typed Notes

Whether or not you write a note by hand is often a matter of personal style and the quality of your penmanship. Certain notes, like condolences and thankyous, should always be written by hand. Handwriting says, "I took the time to sit down and think about what I'm going to say."

A handwritten note can also increase the likelihood that your note will be read. "When I get a hand-addressed envelope, I'll open it. There's something about realizing there's a human being on the other side," says the senior vice president of a major advertising agency.

If your script is sloppy or illegible, or if you're writing a longer note and it will be difficult for people to read your handwriting, use a word processor. Always type a cover letter for a résumé, and always type international correspondence, especially if you are sending it by fax, as typing is usually easier to read. But do sign *all* of your notes personally—in ink, of course.

You can personalize a formal memo or the typed minutes of a meeting or a typed letter by adding to it a few handwritten lines: "It was great to see you at the conference. Marilyn sends her regards," or "Your talk at the distributors' breakfast was dynamite."

Part Two

❦

Strictly Business

3

Follow-up Notes

I got an order yesterday from out of the blue," says the vice president of a confectionery wholesaler. "Since it was a very big order, I was curious about why *I* got the business. I sell a product you can buy anywhere—there's nothing special about mine. So I asked, 'What made you choose us?' The customer told me, 'When I called and asked for information, everyone else sent a brochure. But you sent a brochure *and* you wrote a personal note. That made a difference to me.'"

What did the note say? Nothing earth-shattering—just two handwritten lines:

Dear————,

Many thanks for your inquiry. I'm sure we can meet your needs.

Sincerely,

Whether you're following up a sales call or a request for information, a personal note is a way to encourage someone who is actively interested in your product or service to take the next step by giving the order or signing the contract.

As you can see, a note worked powerfully in this case. "The order was huge, and that's not surprising. The personal touch has all but disappeared today, which is why people sit up and pay attention when they *do* get something personalized," says the vice president, whose business also has one of the highest reorder rates in the industry. "But why *not* write a few lines? It's fun to do, and it feels great when somebody responds like that."

—— • ——

Other situations will also present opportunities to write follow-up notes. Here are some examples, as well as tips on how to put them to work for you.

Meetings and Events

A note to someone you've met at a presentation, meeting, or other event can strengthen a good first impression or enhance an existing relationship. Take the note an international trade attorney wrote after a conference with a potential client:

> *Dear* ——,
> *I enjoyed meeting you. Thought you'd be interested in the enclosed article on trade opportunities in Hong Kong. Look forward to hearing from you.*
> *Regards,*

Says the writer, "I'd just met the person, but I kept the tone casual, since we'd had an instant rapport. I think people are flattered when an attorney takes a friendly tone. People think of a lawyer as 'a stuffy guy who will take all my money and not do anything for me.' Here it turns out he's a regular guy who truly wants to help you."

After meeting a possible source of business at a convention, a stockbroker wrote this note:

Dear ———,

Thought you would like to have these photos as a memento of the Tucson convention.
It was a pleasure to meet you.

Sincerely,

One marketing consultant to corporations carries a camera in his briefcase at all times. When he feels the setting is appropriate, he asks someone to snap a picture of him and someone he's met. Along with the photo, he sends a note saying something like "Thought you'd enjoy this shot of us on the golf course."

"It's very subtle," he says, "and the timing and situation have to be exactly right, but a camera is a wonderful tool. A lot of people have scrapbooks."

Networking connections need reinforcement, too. One vice president of a large public relations firm wrote to a contact and former colleague after a productive session:

Dear ———,

I thoroughly enjoyed our tea for two. Maybe we didn't solve all our problems, but we came darn close. Let's do it again soon.

Regards,

The executive director of a nonprofit organization in the health care field uses notes to woo board members and build a constituency of supporters. For instance, after speaking with someone at a post-meeting reception, the director followed up the next day with "How wonderful it was to see you last night."

Since you never know if people you meet can potentially do you some good, it's also smart to follow up chance encounters outside of work. A company owner often lectures about his hobby locally. After one of his talks, an audience member, who happened to be a business consultant, stayed to ask questions. "He wanted additional information, and I offered to look it up. The next day I found it, made a copy, and mailed it out to him with a note saying, 'Enjoyed meeting you yesterday. I think this is what you were looking for.' A year later the consultant called and said, 'You probably don't remember me, but I was at your lecture last year and you mentioned your company manufactures office furniture. I have a customer who needs some, and I've told him about you. Would you go see him?'

"I made an appointment and called on the customer the following Monday morning. By Thursday I had closed a big order. Soon after that, I got an expansion order for more. All this business because I followed up a year ago."

Thank You for Your Business
Thank-you notes convey that there's more to the relationship than the strictly business aspect. They represent a closure that says, "We value your trust in us,"

which is why you should write them as often as you can. One money manager for high-profile clients remembers receiving this note from a grateful financial vendor:

Dear ———,

Just want to let you know how much we appreciate the business and your confidence in us. If a problem should arise at any time, please call me.

Sincerely,

Says the money manager, "The note came from the boss of the person I dealt with, and it reconfirmed my assessment that they were able to do the job. It was something extra that made me feel they were aware of my concerns. It also gave me another name to call higher up if there was a problem."

The president of an office equipment company sends a thank-you to the customer whenever one of his salesmen sells a job. He'll write:

Dear ———,

We really appreciate your becoming our customer. I look forward to meeting you when the job is installed.

Sincerely,

He views these notes as business builders. "Let's say you buy a refrigerator," he says, "and the salesman sends you a note saying, 'Thanks for selecting my brand. If you have any problems give me a call. Signed John Smith.' What will you do? You'll say, 'Wow, that was unusual.' And you'll tell others about the person.

"If you buy a sport jacket at a clothing store, it's rare

to get a thank-you note," he says. "If the salesman writes, 'Hope you enjoy this good-looking jacket. Thanks for your business,' you remember it. If you could somehow make all your employees courteous and thoughtful, you wouldn't need mega-advertising during the Super Bowl to sell your product."

Some businesses buy printed cards that say, "We appreciate your business." If you normally send one out after a sale, why not add a handwritten line to increase the impact: "Thank you very much for your order. If I can be of any further service, let me know."

Thank You for the Referral

Referrals are a key source of business in fields like accounting, financial and creative services, and law. Notes of appreciation will help keep those important referrals coming.

In one case, someone recommended a real estate agent to a friend who was looking for commercial space. "He did a terrific job for us, so I always mention his name," he said. The agent, who would earn a large commission on the transaction, wrote this note to him:

Dear —————,

Many thanks for referring Bob Cavanaugh to me. I will see that he gets special treatment. I appreciate your thinking of me.

Best,

Even if a referral doesn't pan out, it's smart to say thank you. A partner in an interior design firm wrote:

> *Dear ———,*
>
> *I met with Sam Magorini last Tuesday. He's a very nice guy, but I don't think I can be of help to him.*
>
> *We appreciate the introduction. Please keep us in mind in the future.*
>
> *Best regards,*

Thanks for Advice and Assistance

The purpose of some follow-up notes is to keep an already established and cordial relationship going. Let's say a bank vice president has arranged a line of credit or long-term financing for your company. Says the chief financial officer of a women's sportswear manufacturer, "You write the person a note because next week you might need more money, or something might go wrong and you might be late making a payment. Someone who has a relationship with you is going to be easier to deal with and more likely to cut you some slack."

What can you write? Try something like this:

> *Dear ———,*
>
> *Thank you for your advice and assistance in arranging our line of credit. We look forward to a long and mutually beneficial relationship.*
>
> *Sincerely,*

Or maybe you want to express gratitude for a job done above and beyond the level you'd normally expect, or you want to write because someone has treated you especially well. In one case, a client was terrified of being sued by another company. According to his attorney, "He came to me and said, 'I haven't slept in two years worrying about this matter. I'm afraid I'll be wiped out.' In fact, there was no chance of that, so I told him, 'Don't worry about it. You're not liable.' I generally put his mind at ease."

The client later wrote this note to the lawyer:

Dear ———,

You are a mensch. Thank you for speaking so frankly to me. I've been to three lawyers, and they had me scared half to death.

It's worth everything to know that I'm in such good hands.

Sincerely,

Says the attorney, "I felt flattered. It never hurts to be nice to people. It takes very little effort to say thank you."

A corporate consultant and speaker feels notes are so important that he always carries stamps and note paper when he's traveling. In describing a note he wrote to a hotel manager, he explains, "I was setting up a seminar and needed additional tables and other equipment. The manager had several other meetings going on, but she saw to it that I got everything I needed." The consultant wrote to her immediately:

Dear ———,

Thank you so much for going out of your way to help me set up the seminar today. I know you had a very busy schedule.

> *The level of customer service that I received was extraordinary. I want you to know that I will highly recommend this hotel to other business travelers.*
>
> *It was a pleasure to work with you.*
>
> *Sincerely,*

He added this postscript: "Should you ever see an opportunity where a company needs a speaker, I'd be glad to send materials," and he enclosed his business card with the note.

One of the values of correspondence is that it often winds up in a file somewhere, and it may be reviewed again. He says, "I can think of two speaking engagements I got where the person called me from out of the blue after finding a letter I'd sent."

Always say thank you to someone who has helped you get information. By doing so, you create a connection that you can go back to.

A financial adviser needs to stay current on changes in the law. When she wanted details on a recent change, a colleague pointed her to someone who could provide the answers. She took the time to write:

> *Dear —————,*
>
> *Thank you for the introduction to John Young. He was very knowledgeable, and I appreciate your help.*
>
> *Please let me know if I can return the favor.*
>
> *Best regards,*

If you're active in a trade, professional, or alumni organization or a community or charity activity, you may have to call on others to serve on committees or to organize programs. A thank-you note is more than a courtesy. It also helps ensure that the person will volunteer again.

The president of a professional writers' organization wrote this note to someone who ran a successful symposium:

Dear ————,

> You were the talk of the council meeting last night, and so I thought I ought to put our appreciation in writing.
>
> All of us were thrilled to hear of the great success of your symposium. We were not surprised; after all, you were leading the effort. But we do have an inkling of how much hard work went into this, and we want to send our congratulations and thanks to you and to all the members of your committee. Bravo!
>
> All best wishes,

In addition to praising the person, you can also mention the audience reaction and the success of the entire event, as in this note to someone who moderated a panel at a professional conference:

Dear ————,

> Congratulations on the program! We heard nothing but raves, and it helped boost attendance

at the sessions the next day—a definite plus for
the conference.
  See you later in the month.

                                          Best,

An attorney with a major computer maker sometimes invites a lawyer from another organization to speak to his staff. Afterward, he'll write a note like this one:

Dear ———,
  Thank you for visiting on Thursday and speaking to the staff about contracting skills. Everyone was very pumped up.
  If you're available, I'd like you to be our guest at our kickoff meeting in May. You've played a role in our success this past year.

                                       Regards,

Thank You for the Raise

Sometimes you want to thank your own management. After receiving a handsome salary increase, a young public relations executive wrote to the president of his company:

Dear ———,
  The first time I met you, we exchanged philosophies about the state of the world and ate chocolate chip cookies in your office. I thought to myself, "This place is special."
  After four years, I'm still discovering just how special. Thank you for your generosity.

                                     Sincerely,

To the second-in-command, he wrote:

Dear ———,

I am very touched by your generosity and faith in my abilities. But most of all, I wish to thank you for never allowing public relations to become "just a job."

I am truly fortunate.

Sincerely,

Notes like these will confirm people's positive opinion of you and provide feedback to management as well. Says one boss, "Sitting down and writing a note takes extra effort. Everybody says thank you, but you never really know what the person's true feelings are. A note expresses them. You feel the increase was appreciated and that you pleased your staff."

What if you think you deserve a much larger raise? Write a note about *that,* as in: "I felt my raise did not recognize my contributions. I'd really like to talk to you about how I can better meet your expectations."

4

Stay-in-Touch Notes

If you write a note when there isn't a reason,
you bank a little goodwill.

—Marketing director, large accounting firm

It helps to have a concrete reason to write to people who are important to your business, but you can stay visible and connected by simply *creating* an appropriate reason for a note. This is not difficult to do, but your reason has to make sense: there's a thin line between being welcome and being a pest.

One co-owner of a small company read a very positive article about a customer in a trade paper. He clipped it and sent it to the customer with a note consisting of two words: "Flattering article!"

"They're one of my biggest accounts now," he says. "Everyone else read the article, too, but to me it registered. My note lets them know that *I* know they did a good job. Everyone likes good publicity, and everyone likes to be acknowledged. Why not let people know you value them?"

When you haven't heard from a customer or a referral source in a while, it's always smart to send a note.

One of the best ideas is to tie it in with a report or other information that may be of interest to the person. Send the report along with a note saying something like "Thought you'd want to see this. Haven't heard from you lately. How about lunch next week to catch up?" If you're writing to a retail customer, close with "I'd love to see you. Please stop by."

One sales manager feels so strongly about targeted stay-in-touch notes to customers that he talks about them at sales meetings. "I say to my salesmen, 'What do you like to get back? That someone remembers you and knows who you are.'

"Let's say I'm a dog-lover. What's the best thing I could get in the mail? An interesting article or other information about dogs. Why? The fact that you know I love dogs and you absorbed that and remembered my interest says, 'I'm listening to you.' You took the time to send it and write across the top, 'Hey, Joe, here's something for you,' and that says, 'I may not know very much about dogs myself, but I respect you and I know *you* do.'

"Some say that's contrived or manipulative," he says. "I don't think it is. I think it's being friendly and doing somebody a favor. People are always willing to work with someone who's friendly."

Look for mutual interests and ask yourself what you can talk about besides your product. Often you can pass along things *you've* received in the mail. Are you and a customer both crazy about the theater? Send the announcement of a new production with a brief note:

> *Dear* —————,
>
>   *I think you'll enjoy this. I saw it in previews,*
>   *and it kept me riveted.*
>
> *Best,*

Do you know someone who loves to go on cruises? When you get a brochure in the mail about riverboat excursions or cruises to Alaska, seize the opportunity. Send it with a note:

> *Dear* —————,
>
>   *Thought this was your kind of trip.*
>
> *Regards,*

Is a director of a data processing center a gourmet cook? Think of all the recipes and restaurant recommendations you can send. When you especially enjoy eating at a new restaurant, pick up a card on your way out and enclose it with your note. Some restaurants and wine merchants occasionally mail newsletters to customers. They're perfect pass-alongs, too.

Does a client share your passion for goldfish ponds? Send along your new water lily catalog with a personal note that says:

> *Dear* —————,
>
>   *Don't know if you've seen this, but it's hard to*
>   *resist. I've already ordered plenty, so you can*
>   *keep it.*
>
> *Regards,*

One accountant refers to notes as "tickets to the top." He'll see an article in a tax bulletin or newspaper that affects someone and immediately mail it out. He even sent a clip to someone who had chosen a competing firm over his own. "I didn't get him as a client, but I'd seen him two weeks earlier and recalled that he had to hire a bookkeeper. I wrote, 'I came across this ad and thought you'd be interested.'"

Why write to someone who *won't* be your client? "Because he'll remember it as an extra special effort," the accountant says. "Who knows? If his choice doesn't work out and he's looking for an accountant again, or if a friend asks him to recommend someone, maybe he'll say, 'You know, I went with someone else, but this guy really impressed me.' Who knows where a note can eventually lead?"

Nurturing Contacts

Notes are also a way to stay in touch with your peers in your line of work. Being able to obtain data from them—when you need it—can help you hold the line on costs. Says an executive, "We all have the best intentions of calling people, but I can't stay on the phone all week talking about what's selling, what's creative, what others are doing, what people are asking for. If you keep the relationship up mainly with notes, people will take your occasional and important call."

A manager who travels a great deal and loves to stay in touch says, "I write notes because I like to get notes from others. Note-writing has taken on a much more personal aspect because of the way we live today. We can just dash something off on the computer or fax it. When a note comes in the mail, it's like finding a little gem in there. The reaction is, 'Oh look, it's a note from Pat. I haven't heard from her lately.'"

This manager writes to eight former co-workers who now work for competitors or have changed fields. "They send me postcards wherever they go, and I send them cards," says the manager. "I'll write, 'Here I am in San Francisco. I visited Paula Kirk. I stayed at the Fairmont. Everyone deserves a weekend at the Fairmont.' Then when I call and want to get a sales figure, there's no feeling of having been out of touch. You can often get a genuine back-and-forth going."

Another way to stay in touch is to ask yourself how you can be useful to someone. Did the person mention looking for a reading light? Clip and send the ad you saw.

Dear ———,

I found this ad in a catalog, and it seems close to what you're looking for.

How is the Florida project progressing? Let me know.

Best of luck!

If lunch or dinner conversation turns to a particular book, a banker often sends a copy to the person with a note. "I just sent one guy a book on ethics that we'd talked about," he says.

An executive maintains contact with a very simple note: "I was thinking of you today. It's been so long since we got together, and I just wanted to connect." She says, "Even if they look at it and throw it in the wastebasket, they say, 'Yeah, there's Mary.' It's a reminder that you're still around."

One company uses status reports to keep in touch with customers. Says the president, "During the course of a project that's very detailed, we'll send progress reports to our customers. It's a way to cover ourselves and make sure our clients are aware of what we're doing. But also, isn't it nice when you're spending $50,000 to know the status of the project rather than have to call and say, 'Is this stuff going to be on time?' It's also nice on Monday morning to get a note from this company that says, 'Dear Mr. Jones, Here's the status of your project. We plan to be there on Thursday, and everything is going well.'"

You can use notes to transmit news about problems, and the sooner you deal with them the better. Says one company president, "Like any business, we sometimes have to deliver bad news. I've found you should address it as soon as you can and make the customer aware of it. To your status note you might add, 'By the way, we do have one problem.' And you tell them what steps you're taking to solve it. Most customers can live with it if I write in advance, 'We have a problem here due to a vendor's failure to supply the product on time. We may be a day or two late. I'll keep you advised.'"

But the tone of your note should depend on the nature of the message. "If you write, 'Dear Client, We've just lost the case. Enclosed please find my bill,' the client thinks you never cared about him at all," says an attorney who specializes in securities law. "What you should say is, 'Despite all our best efforts, we lost. Here are the choices you now have.'

50

"There are inappropriate ways to convey bad news. Truly terrible news—for example, 'You lost the case, you're going to jail'—should never be sent by mail. The worse the news, the more appropriate it is to deliver it in person, face-to-face."

The Travel Excuse

Travel is a wonderful reason to write stay-in-touch notes, and you can mention their vacation—or yours if you wish. Did someone talk about a recent holiday in England? Try something like this:

Dear ———,
I just came across this article on Wales and thought you'd enjoy it. Maybe another trip?
Sincerely,

Who doesn't enjoy receiving a postcard from Paris or Bermuda? What can you write? Instead of talking all about yourself and what you're doing, keep mentioning the other person, as in "I know you're a skier and you'd love these Alps."

Discuss the meals, both good and bad, the hotels, the scenery, and the interesting history, but always tie your message in to the recipient. Discuss the lush plantings at Fontainebleau to a garden lover. Travel calamities are always of interest to people who know you well. Did the automated gas pump in Switzerland eat your credit card, leaving you stranded? Write about it. Chances are, the recipient will chuckle and mention it when you return.

5

Notes to Celebrate and Motivate

Recognizing Promotions, Awards,
and Other Achievements

Words of congratulations and recognition build goodwill both inside and outside your company —and writing a note is a nice thing to do. "It feels terrific to know you're not working in a vacuum," says an executive who designs computer software. Here's how to convey the message "I noticed what you did" and sound as if you really mean it.

You see notices like these in the newspapers and business press all the time:

- In the latest personnel shift in the volatile film industry, Thomas Jones will take the helm of Circle Corp.

- Cynthia Parks was named director of strategic planning for Granaco.

- Barry Anderson of Woods and Klein has won the Silver Trophy Award for 1997.

Perhaps an announcement of a move arrives in the mail or you hear about other good news through the grapevine. If you know the person and think, "Good for her," but then forget it, you've missed a chance to make an impact.

In the case of a friend, you feel genuinely happy for the person and want to extend your good wishes. A thoughtful note to an acquaintance can advance a relationship or rekindle a potentially useful one from the past. Even if someone moves out of the industry or the department, in the future that person could become a source of business or even an employer. Some people climb quickly to the top and could hire you at their new company.

But keep in mind that just "congratulations" won't do. You'll want to express admiration and support and show respect for the person's accomplishment; it's important to write something appropriate. If you've known each other for years, your words can reflect that fact. A vice president in charge of finance wrote this note to an old friend who had planned to retire but instead wound up president of a division of a bank:

> Dear ———,
>   *Retirement certainly turned out to be different from what you expected. Congratulations!*
>   *Regards,*

Says the writer, "I tried to say something that would make my friend remember me and smile. Anyone can write, 'Congratulations on your new job.' *This* note says, 'We've been friends a long time.'"

You can also talk about special qualities that have contributed to the change, like assertiveness, leadership skills, or vision, as in: "Few people possess your talent for no-nonsense decision-making." An all-purpose line can come in handy, too—"Cream always rises to the top," for example.

Discuss the investment the person has made—in going back to graduate school, for example, or relocating to a new city. If this is someone you've mentored, you can mention your feelings: "I'm so proud of you."

Promotions

An advancement is validation of a job well done, and you'll want to reflect that in your note: "Bravo! I'm impressed" or "You deserve it." When a contact was appointed to a top post in a government agency after working his way up through the ranks, a lobbyist wrote:

Dear ———,
    This appointment is long overdue. You've always stood out from the pack in intelligence, initiative, and ability to lead and manage people. You're going to give the Department of Commerce a shot in the arm.

                    Warm congratulations,

What do you say when you're uncertain whether a job change is a promotion or a lateral move? One executive wrote:

Dear ———,
    I just learned of your new assignment, and I could not be happier. At long last they've

appointed someone who has the experience and
knowledge to do the job right.

    A congratulatory dinner is certainly in order.
I'll call you next week to set a date.

Best wishes,

It's standard practice in many companies to post announcements of internal promotions or to send a memo around. The latter is usually a congratulatory message as well as an announcement. If you have to write one, take the time to make it special. A vice president asked co-workers and clients, "What do you think of Pete Johansen?" He began the promotion announcement like this: "This is a memo that writes itself. Pete has done a great job. Let's congratulate him on his promotion. Need I say more?" He then used some of the quotes. Snippets included "Pete is great to work with" and "Pete always comes through with an original concept."

How did the recipient react? "It made me feel good to know people enjoyed working with me," he says. "It was clever and pertinent to have all those compliments crossing my desk—and everyone else's."

Changing Companies or Careers

When someone leaves for other opportunities, you can say, "You'll be missed," talk about your connections, and stress that you hope to preserve these ties. An attorney who had worked with an executive at an electronics company for years learned this individual would be leaving. They shared a love of black humor and had called each other regularly to repeat the latest jokes. The attorney wrote:

Dear ————,

Congratulations and best of luck. With your ability, I'm certain you'll have great success at Polycorp.

Your creativity and ingenuity have always impressed me. When I am about to pick up the phone to talk to you, I always smile for two reasons: at least one new joke is on the way—and I know you'll ask a question or broach a matter that will test my wits. Don't spread this around, but there were times I so enjoyed our conversations that you could have billed me!

It is difficult to imagine the company without you, but it is impossible to imagine my not hearing from you in the future. So let's keep in touch.

Warmly,

A sales manager for a pharmaceutical company wrote this note to a colleague:

Dear ————,

I learned today that you are leaving to start a new career in corporate finance. I'm not surprised that you've had the intelligence and determination to make the move.

I wish you the best of luck, though I am fully aware that your departure is the company's loss as well as my own. I have been fortunate to work *with some outstanding people during my twenty-two years with this company, and you certainly rank up there at the top.*

I look forward to seeing you again in the future.
All the best,

When a former colleague launched a new magazine, an advertising manager wrote her a note that showed he appreciated the enormity of the undertaking:

Dear ———,

I saw the write-up in the Daily Banner *today. It sounds fabulous, and if anyone can make a new magazine a winner, you* can. *I'll be looking for it on the newsstands. Here's to success ahead.*
Regards,

For someone else taking a chance, how about starting with this quote from the Russian politician Aleksandr I. Lebed: "He who doesn't take risks doesn't drink champagne." You might follow with "I have every confidence in your success."

Was someone elected to the state legislature or the town board? One person wrote:

Dear ———,

This is so exciting! I've always known how capable and smart you are. Now the rest of the population does, too. There's no doubt you're going to do a great job for your constituents. You'd better—I'm one of them!

Best wishes,

Moving or Opening an Office

It takes a major effort—intellectual, emotional, and financial—to plan and prepare to relocate an office. You need to notify customers, coordinate and reorganize business activities, and work with movers and landlords. Why not mention your awareness of what the change involves?

A sales representative wrote this note to a friend who had just moved:

> *Dear ———,*
>
> *You're finally there! Best of luck in the new location. When you're settled, I'll call to schedule one of our great lunches—like old times.*
>
> *Best regards,*

When one firm took a risk and moved its offices to a less than prime section of town, a friend and client sent a handsome plant and wrote this note:

> *Dear ———,*
>
> *Congratulations! You've always been a pioneer and had the best judgment. You're starting a trend, I'm sure.*
>
> *Best of luck,*

Special Achievements and Awards

Is someone you know in the spotlight? Drop him a note to convey your pleasure that something wonderful has happened to him:

> *Dear* ————,
>
>   *Just heard about your award from the*
>   *Chamber of Commerce. It's about time you*
>   *were recognized. We're so proud to know you.*
>   *Congratulations.*
>
> *Best,*

You can also mention where you heard the news. While on vacation, an electronics company executive sent a picture postcard to an engineer friend that said, "Here I am, enjoying my morning coffee and reading the newspaper in Santa Fe, when I see that you just won this year's Patent Excellence Award. Congratulations!"

When the president of a professional organization fought for and won a big concession from her industry that would benefit all the members, the achievement was announced in the newspapers. A colleague sent the clip to her, writing across the top:

> *Dear* ————,
>
>   *Good for you! You've done a tremendous job.*
>   *This couldn't have happened without you. I*
>   *admire you more than I can say.*
>
> *All the best,*

Other Reasons to Write

Sometimes you want to express support for someone who is *trying* to advance. One young investment banker was competing for a promotion and had one interview that went poorly. He spoke about the experience to a friend and colleague, who wrote:

Dear ———,

I just wanted to tell you that I admire what you're doing. Remember that it's the irritants in the oyster that make the pearl. Let me know how it all turns out.

Sincerely,

When you want to encourage someone, how about sending along this quote from Gilbert and Sullivan's *Ruddigore*:

> If you wish in this world to advance,
> Your merits you're bound to enhance.
> You must stir it and stump it
> And blow your own trumpet,
> Or, trust me, you haven't a chance.

Even if the words in your message *don't* rhyme, the fact that you cared enough to take the time to write will mean a lot to people.

Employee Recognition

Recognition is a very important motivator to most people, but companies tend to do a pretty poor job of giving it to employees.

—*Psychologist*

I think a carrot's a much better management tool
than a stick. I work better when praised. I think
everybody does. It's a very effective way to get
people to do their best work.

—Senior vice president

Paychecks, perks, and benefits encourage loyalty and
motivate people. But words of praise count, too, if you
want to keep employees committed and happy. Recognition makes people feel like members of a team. It
can even save money in the long run, because morale
problems undermine productivity. Employee turnover
is expensive, especially when you've invested time and
money in training, and good people can be hard to
find. Notes are one way to let employees know how
much they're appreciated.

Says one corporate consultant, "I've counseled managers to write more notes. It's nice to have someone
says 'attaboy' or 'attagirl,' but it's much more powerful
to receive a letter of commendation from your boss or a
note acknowledging achievement."

One senior manager for an international cosmetics
company believes thank-you notes to employees should
be an ingrained part of business procedure. "Most people, especially those in middle management and up,
never hear words of appreciation from anyone—their
own bosses included. Management's main effort is to
get its best people to work the hardest, to encourage
those people to be the most productive and loyal, and
to pay them the least money. They don't realize the

benefits they'd reap if they would thank people at the end of the day. Imagine a vice president writing to a director, 'I know it was a tough week, and I want you to know what a fine job you did in handling all the loose ends. Thank you.'"

This same manager frames his own notes thoughtfully and tries to focus on a specific incident. He explains, "You have to write more than just 'thank you.' Otherwise your note doesn't mean a whole lot. In only ten words you can say, 'Thank you for a dynamic presentation. It really excited everyone.' Or you can write a slightly longer message: 'I can't tell you how effective your training was. You've given me a deeper insight into the business. Thank you.' Personalizing each note will take a few minutes of your time, but the results will be worth the effort."

Did someone's suggestion save a project? How about sending this acknowledgment:

Dear ————,

The ideas you submitted the other day made the difference for this project. It wouldn't have succeeded without your creativity. Keep up the good work.

Best,

Some bosses regularly attach thoughtful notes to their employees' paychecks. One writes every month to a store manager something like this: "Wishing you the best. I hope your wife is well." Does this kind of note really count? It does to the recipient, who said, "Please don't stop writing them."

The owner of a small company often writes compliments on paycheck stubs, using one-liners like "Thanks for the great job you did with Jackson Products." This is a good place to write because most people keep their pay stubs as a record. "My notes always astonish new employees," he says. "At first, they think they're going to be reprimanded or criticized, either about something they neglected to do or something they did wrong. Imagine their reactions when what they get is a thank-you for a job well done."

He also writes notes on reports from employees, jotting a line or two on the cover page—for instance, "This is a great idea, but I have a few questions to ask. I'd like to talk to you on Wednesday." He explains, "There's a subtle difference between that and taking a fresh piece of paper. When they get a report back with a note like this, they know I have really looked at it."

Relay Compliments

Another way to recognize employees is to pass along praise from others outside the company. Did a satisfied customer call to say, "Dan worked like a beaver to satisfy our needs," or "Our job's coming up. Could we have Jerry install it?" Transmit that information not only to the person who has been singled out for praise but to everyone behind that person who put the product or project together.

When a client called a public relations firm to praise the work of an account executive, the executive's boss sent her this note:

Dear ———,

Kudos from Tom Geary. He called to say how impressed he was with the job you did.

Regards,

"It was just a two-line memo," said the account executive, "but it made me feel recognized. I learned from it. Now I always thank people who work for me. I'll write, 'Just wanted to let you know how pleased I am with the way you handled the project. Well done!' I send copies to everyone, including my own boss and the president of the company."

Someone else wrote:

Dear ———,

I talked to Fred from Heller Bros., and I want you to know he really appreciated your contribution in getting this packaging delivered on time. Thank you.

All the best,

Many corporations give incentives and awards in recognition of employees' work and effort. The reward might be anything from a fifty-dollar gift certificate for a restaurant to a check for a more significant amount. One manager wrote this note to a member of his staff:

Dear ———,

Thank you for your outstanding contribution to the RMG contract this year. An achievement award for $750 is on the way.
Congratulations!

Sincerely,

The Payoff

"If you treat people with respect, they'll go out of their way for you," says the managing partner in a law firm. "My secretary usually works from nine to five, but last night she said, 'I'll stay late to finish the bills.' Normally you have to ask, 'Would you stay?' But obviously she feels some obligation to us, because she recognizes that she's an important part of our team. I think it's because I go out of my way to let her know she makes a difference."

The next morning the partner sent her this E-mail message: "I really appreciate your taking the time to clean up the bills. Thank you."

How do your employees view themselves? Are they working *for* you or *with* you? Says the law firm partner, "You want people to feel they're contributing something. When I get a nice piece of work from an associate, I send a note saying, 'You did a good job on this.'"

The key word, however, is "good." You don't want to overdo praise. It's one thing to recognize someone for reaching a sales goal, another to send out so many notes to your staff that they lose their meaning.

Says a psychologist and corporate consultant, "It's like constantly telling your spouse, 'I love you.' There's an optimal number of times to do that. You have to be careful that it doesn't become automatic or insincere."

6

Notes for Retirement, Job Loss, and Resignation

Some people anticipate leaving the business world or a particular company with pleasure. As one door closes, another one full of promise and possibilities opens. In other cases, departure may be involuntary and future prospects unappealing or uncertain. Whatever the nature of the transition, you may want to write a personal note, and what you say will, as always, depend on the circumstances and on your relationship with the recipient.

Retirement

Retirement is a milestone in any career. It's also the beginning of a new phase of life, bringing with it changes in status, roles, and lifestyle. In a note you can pay tribute to the person and talk about his accomplishments and his contribution to the organization. An accountant wrote this note to her senior partner:

Dear ———,

You've been a mentor, a friend, and a role model. I don't think anyone will match your accomplishments. Your rainmaking abilities have helped the firm triple in size.

This place won't be the same without you. Be assured that we will seek your advice in the future.

Have a long and happy retirement.

                                        Best of luck,

When an interior designer retired, a long-standing client wrote this note:

Dear ———,

It's hard to imagine renovating the office and not handing the job over to you. You are truly unique.

Your good taste and endless patience have always made working with you a pleasure. You've made both my work space and my home elegant and supremely comfortable.

I wish you well.

                                        Warmly,

P.S. Will you be available for touch-ups?

Humor is very effective when you know the person well. After a trade paper article announced that a CEO client and friend was retiring after fourteen years with the company, a consultant enclosed the clipping and wrote:

Dear ———,

> *Many people on your staff will swear under oath that you retired fourteen years ago!*
>
> *I would very much like to take you out for a nice leisurely lunch, at which time we can toast this auspicious occasion. Please ask your secretary to let me know when you're free.*
>
> *All good wishes,*

For a more serious tone, the writer could have changed the first sentence to "Given your contributions to the company, it's hard to believe you've been there only fourteen years."

Write about the person's retirement plans, which can run the gamut from a new career to volunteer work or further education to pursuing a hobby or puttering around the house. The president of a packaging company received this note from an industry colleague:

Dear ———,

> *Nobody deserves a rest more than you do, after fifty years in the business. I know you've wanted to live in a warmer climate for a long time and to travel and play more golf and bridge.*
>
> *I'm glad you're finally doing what makes you happy. However, your retirement makes me unhappy. It is the industry's loss.*
>
> *All the best,*

When a government official retired at fifty-six, someone who often dealt with him focused on his personal qualities:

Dear ———,

It has been a while since we last spoke, so the news of your retirement came as a surprise. Sitting on a rocker on the porch wouldn't suit you, so I hope that you have plans for much bigger and better things.

Anyone who ever dealt with you knows what a thoughtful and considerate person you are. It was always comforting to know that no matter how far off the wall my ideas were, I would get a fair hearing from you. Thanks for your patience and good humor.

All the best to you and your family for the future.

Warmly,

Retirement can also be an opportunity to express gratitude to someone for help in the past. An executive wrote this note to a superior she'd worked closely with:

Dear ———,

Over the years you've given me support and counsel that were incredibly valuable to me. I wish you well in your future endeavors. If there is ever anything I can do, please let me know.

Warmly,

Be Sensitive

When people retire at age sixty-five or beyond, it's usually because they've come to a natural end of a career. They've earned retirement, and there's often much celebration. But some people really don't want to retire; they're leaving due to company policy or for medical or other reasons. In such cases your note should focus on how the person will be missed or on work achievements. If appropriate, add, "Let's stay in touch." That message can mean a great deal to someone who's unhappy about retirement.

Job Loss

"A major company just laid off two hundred people in our city," says a psychologist who advises corporations. "These people will be out of a job, feeling shocked and alienated. If you know anyone in a situation like that, realize that when such a difficult thing happens, people need to hear from others."

Those who get downsized or laid off frequently face a financial and emotional crisis. Friends and colleagues often don't write because they don't know what to say, yet it's devastating when the person doesn't hear from anyone. It makes a difference even if you write only a few words, such as "Just want you to know I'm thinking of you. Let me know if there's something I can do."

A personal note is not only the kind thing to do; it's smart. People eventually wind up somewhere else where they may be able to help *you*—and they'll remember your thoughtfulness.

What can you write when you know the other person probably feels devastated?

Acknowledge what has happened. It's important to express compassion and say, in effect, "You've taken a tough shot. This is a terrible thing that's occurred." You recognize the other person's loss and show empathy by saying, "I realize what a terrible blow this must be." You might write something like this: "John, I really feel for you. We're with you," or "People are in your corner. Hang in there."

Express your shock. The words "I don't know what to say" are extremely powerful because they acknowledge that you're shocked, too. They validate what the person is experiencing.

If you've had a similar experience, you can say, "I understand because I was laid off myself last month. I know how difficult this is." But don't follow that up with a long story about what happened to you. Also, it's best not to say, "I understand *totally.*" Everyone reacts differently. You can't *completely* understand other people's experiences, and you can't assume anything about their reaction.

Offer support. The support you offer doesn't have to be tangible; it can be emotional support in the form of "Let's have lunch next Tuesday and I'll lend an ear." Just letting the person sound off really does help. A large part of what outplacement firms do is soak up some of the anger felt by people who have been fired. Then they can discharge it at somebody safe, rather than venting it at the boss, who may be needed for a reference later.

If you feel comfortable about it, you can offer to let the person tap into your network and your Rolodex, or you can write a third-party letter and send the person's résumé to someone who may be helpful. When writing such a letter you might say something like this:

Dear ————,

I'm enclosing a copy of a friend's résumé. He's a first-class auditor who just lost his job.

If you hear of or know of an available position in his field, please feel free to give him a call.

Regards,

Resignation

The note you write to someone who has resigned depends on their reason for departure. If the person is leaving for a new and better job elsewhere, congratulations are appropriate. You'll write something different, however, if the circumstances are less than celebratory.

In one case, a young man's resignation was due to a stand on principle. A colleague in the industry wrote:

Dear ————,

It takes guts to stick to what you believe in. I have no doubt that you'll be quickly snapped up by a company that thinks globally.

I'd like to get together with you before you go. Are you free for lunch next Friday?

Best,

When a personality clash with the firm's partner led an interior decorator to resign, a colleague wrote:

Dear ———,

You've always had class and creativity, and I'm going to miss you. I valued your advice and enjoyed our long discussions about the industry.

Please stay in touch and let me know your future plans.

Sincerely,

If you don't know the exact reason for the resignation but still want to show your support, try something like this:

Dear ———,

I'm sorry things didn't work out at the XYZ Agency. If you need temporary space, I have a desk and telephone available. You're welcome to them. Give me a call.

Knowing you, it won't be long before you find another challenge.

Best,

Another option:

Dear ———,

I just heard the news. What a loss for James, Heller & Ames. Nobody has given more to the firm than you have. It's difficult to think of the place without you.

Let me know what's next.

Regards,

If *you're* the one who's leaving, keep your letter of resignation short, businesslike, and positive. Mention the date you will leave, the reason, and the ways in which you've benefited from working there, as this art director did:

Dear ———,

It is with bittersweet feelings that I announce my resignation from FRZ as of June 30. It's a decision tinged with regret.

I will always have special feelings for the people there. But at this point in my career, I feel that greater challenges and opportunities present themselves elsewhere.

Thank you for having faith in me, nurturing my talent, and pushing me to excel at a difficult craft. I am certain that our paths will cross again in the future.

Sincerely,

You don't want to sound critical because your comments about the company or the people you've worked with could boomerang later when you need a reference. Also, you never know who'll wind up where. Someone could be in a position to help or hurt you in the future. Why make enemies?

It may not be easy to write an upbeat letter of resignation when you intensely dislike your boss or when your time on the job has been say consistent torture. But without shading the truth, you can say: "I enjoyed working with my associates" or "I gained great experience at the company." You can always find *something* positive to write.

7

Notes for Job Seekers

Whether you're employed and interested in changing jobs or out of work and hunting for employment, a good cover letter or a thoughtful note can help you get where you want to be. Here are some guidelines on how to write notes and letters that will help distinguish you from the rest of the pack in a competitive job market.

Cover Letters for Résumés

The purpose of a cover letter is to make a good impression and to generate enough interest to make the reader want to take a look at the enclosed résumé. Your letter should be brief and to the point. Most importantly, it should inspire the reader to take the next step and make contact with you.

There are two basic types of cover letters: customized and non-customized. The non-customized letter takes a generic approach and says, "Are you looking for someone with my kind of experience?" It is sent to a list of companies you might want to work for. Most experts caution against such letters because the response rate is usually extremely low. As one outplacement expert says, "You can send out 1,500 letters and résumés and wind up with only two replies. That's a response of less than 1 percent."

A customized letter is far more effective. It targets a particular position within a company and includes *specific* information about your qualifications for that job. Send this kind of letter when answering an ad (an option which brings up to a 5 percent return) or when writing to someone who you know has a position open at this time.

Elements of a Customized Letter

Your cover letter is a sales tool, and the product you are selling is yourself. To succeed, you first have to do your homework and research the company you're targeting. Head for the library and check out publications that evaluate companies, like *Standard & Poor's*. Study business publications like the *Wall Street Journal* and *Forbes*. Information is also available through trade associations and on the Internet. If possible, obtain a copy of the company's latest annual report; it will provide you with the kind of detailed and up-to-date information you want. If you've been referred to a specific firm, the person who sent you may be able to give you some background information about the company. When you're armed with this type of knowledge, you can refer to it in your cover letter. According to one executive recruiter, "People are always impressed when you mention that you noticed something in the company's annual report."

Organize what you want to say, and keep your letter short—never more than one page. Use formal but simple and precise language. People who try too hard to write eloquently usually turn out something forced and artificial instead.

For a general guideline, follow this three-paragraph model:

Paragraph 1: This is the only shot you have to grab the reader's attention, and you have only a sentence or two in which to do it. One good way to get noticed is to mention the name of the person who referred you. In your first sentence you might say, "Charley Jones suggested I write to you regarding the position of account executive." If you don't have a specific referral, mention an accomplishment of yours that would be of value to the company. These devices will help create a reason for the interviewer to see you.

If you're answering an ad, refer to what the ad says. Is the firm looking for a salesperson with experience in marketing and knowledge of a particular territory? You might say something like "You're looking for a sales executive experienced in marketing and familiar with the New York City metropolitan area. I have successfully sold and marketed consumer services and have lived in northern New Jersey for twenty years."

Tasteful humor can sometimes work, too. Take the following example of a burned-out attorney who quit his job as an assistant D.A. for a quiet life in the country. A few years later, ready for a comeback, the lawyer wrote to his former boss, "I have decided to return to a life of crime."

Now, *that's* a great opening.

Paragraph 2: Focus on how you and your skills can be a match for what the company is looking for. Talk specifically about how you can make an important contribution to the firm. Don't just say, "I'm a good salesperson." Say something quantifiable, as in "Last year I increased our region's sales by 20 percent." Briefly mention some relevant skills, such as expertise in client relationships or computer networks.

If you've learned a company is making a technology shift and you have specific skills that can help them through it, you can say something like this: "I've done this before, I've done it under budget, I've done it on time—and I can do it for you."

An outplacement executive gives this advice: "We suggest leaving plenty of white space and using bulleted lists when appropriate. This will make it easier for readers to pick out the information you want them to focus on."

Paragraph 3: Reinforce the idea that your experience will help the company, and remember that the goal of the cover letter is to get an interview. End your letter with a sentence like this: "I'll call you on November 15 to discuss an appointment for an interview"—and make sure to call on that day. Sign off with "Sincerely" or "Very truly yours."

It's not appropriate to mention salary in your cover

letter. You can discuss that topic in your face-to-face meeting.

If possible, find the name of an individual to whom you can address your letter. Blind ads can be misleading; they sometimes don't even mention the name of the company. "If there is no name, it's safest to address your letter to the Human Resources department," says an executive recruiter.

Writing to Recruiters

When you're writing to a search firm rather than directly to an employer, keep in mind that these companies can get fifty or a hundred unsolicited résumés a day. "In my business, anything is better than a cold call or an unsolicited résumé," says one recruiter. "The number of people I've placed through unsolicited résumés is zero. The people I pay attention to have been referred by someone I know." While it's unrealistic to expect an immediate response, there are a few things you can do to improve your chances of standing out from the pack.

Tell the recruiter what you do at the beginning of your letter, as in "I am currently a vice president of marketing at a large teaching hospital in Chicago, and I am writing at the suggestion of Peter Kim." Avoid statements like "I've heard you are an excellent health care recruiting firm." "I hate that sentence," says one recruiter, "because you don't know the first thing about my firm—and you know it and I know it."

No matter who you're writing to, the wrong way to start is by saying, "I am leaving my present company and looking for a new and challenging position." You're not looking for another company to challenge you; you're looking to add value to *their* bottom line. It's not their job to challenge you or make you happy, although that may happen.

Résumés by Fax or E-Mail

Regardless of the medium used, the goal of your cover letter remains the same: to create interest and to encourage the recipient to remember you. Since many search firms and some companies scan résumés into computer files, they may prefer that you follow up a fax, which is not scannable, or E-mail, with hard copy. Such a follow-up is a good idea, too, because résumés can get misplaced and it's always wise to have backup.

Thank You for the Interview

After you've been interviewed it's absolutely necessary to send a thank-you note. Not only is it the right thing to do, it is another chance to say "Remember me" and to pitch yourself again. Since not all candidates write thank-you notes, it's a way to remind the person that you really want this job. Simply thank your interviewer and express a desire to go forward with the process. Then briefly recap your discussion, and end your note by saying, "Please contact me if you have any other questions."

One candidate, who later landed the job, wrote this short note: "Thank you for seeing me on Thursday. The management of Burke & Clark and the people I've met are truly impressive. I'm very interested in the position and know I can do a good job for you. I will welcome a chance to talk further."

One human resources executive says, "I like a relatively short thank-you; in most cases, all the relevant information has already been shared. But do include something about how you felt, such as 'My interview with Joe was particularly motivating.'"

Other experts prefer longer, more detailed thank-you letters that reiterate why you're a match. Ultimately the length of the note is your own decision. Either way, however, pay careful attention at the interview so that you can mention in your thank-you letter the topics you discussed. "Drop in something to let them know that you were interested in what they were saying. You might even enclose a relevant clip," says a consultant. Write within twenty-four hours while the interview is still fresh in the interviewer's mind.

Some interviewers like to receive handwritten notes. Others prefer something more formal on 8½- by 11-inch paper, similar to a cover letter for a résumé. "It's a matter of opinion," says one expert. "You have to assess which format the recipient is likely to respond to better. But what's important here is to send that note . . . *that's* what matters. I recommend a note that is handwritten in blue-black ink with a fountain pen on a Crane's card. It's hard to get much classier than that."

Always address your thank-yous to "Mr." or "Ms." unless the interviewer asked you to call him by his first name during the interview. In such a case it's up to you whether to say, "Dear Joe" or "Dear Mr. Smith."

Thank You for the Rejection

Even if you don't get the job, it's smart to follow up any interview with a note. That contact might be useful to you in the future, and a thank-you note says, "Keep me in mind in case something else opens up."

Says one seasoned career adviser, "If you were granted an interview, the company must have been interested in you. Only a tiny percentage of people write thank-you notes, and it's impressive to receive this kind of follow up. Sometimes there's a fine distinction between you and someone else. You can say something like 'Thank you for informing me of your decision. Though I'm disappointed I didn't get the position, I remain actively interested in your organization. Please keep my résumé on file.'"

One young woman who didn't get a position that she competed for elsewhere in her company wrote this note:

Dear ———,

I want to thank you for the opportunity to interview for the internship program.

Though I was not accepted, I did appreciate the chance to participate, and I enjoyed meeting you. The process was a valuable experience.

I hope our paths will cross in the future at MAF.

Sincerely,

Writing to Networking Contacts

Networking friends can offer you access to their connections and pass your résumé on to someone else you might not ordinarily be able to reach. It's a good idea to make them aware of your search so they can let you know if they hear of anything. If they offer to help, follow up.

Did you just run into an old acquaintance at an industry event? Write a short note:

Dear ———,

It was so nice to meet you at the sales conference in San Diego. It's been a long time since we worked together at Peters Corp., and I enjoyed catching up.

I appreciate your offer to help me in my job search. I'm enclosing a copy of my résumé. Please keep it on file—just in case.

Again, thanks.

Sincerely,

This note establishes a common bond—the event you both attended—and reactivates your connection, which may someday be helpful. It's the kind of note that creates a positive feeling about you, and you never know what it can lead to. Two weeks later Bob might get a call saying, "I'm looking for a new cost accounting manager, and I don't know anybody. I guess I'll have to put an ad in the paper." This will give Bob the chance to reply, "An old friend of mine is a really good cost accounting manager. I have a copy of his résumé. Why don't I send it to you?"

Appearances

Always remember that you make an impression not only with content but with presentation as well. "You can cut your own throat by sending a sloppy cover letter or thank-you note with misspellings or other errors," warns one executive recruiter. "When people are trying to evaluate a job candidate, they have so little to go on that even the most superficial things can give them an opportunity to make a negative assessment. Every detail is magnified."

Never send a cover letter or a thank-you note on your current employer's stationery. It's in poor taste for you to use the company's paper to get yourself another job.

Part Three

❧

Business-Social

8

Notes for Birthdays, Weddings, Births, and Other Joyous Occasions

I've been to four weddings and a fiftieth birthday party in the last two months—all business-related," says a senior manager at a leading advertising agency. Though his schedule is unusually heavy, we all get invited to celebrate significant events in people's lives. A personal line added to a card or to your note says, "I'm not just a person you do business with. I'm also someone who cares about you as a human being."

Birthdays

Attitudes toward employees' and co-workers' birthdays vary, depending on the size of the organization or department, company policy, and personal preferences. At some companies, you get the day off on your birthday. Whatever your employer's practice is, you will probably not write a birthday note to a customer or contact unless the birthday is a milestone or you're invited to a party.

Some executives never acknowledge office-related

birthdays, viewing them as private matters. Others see them as an opportunity to bond and build morale.

"I spend more time with my co-workers than with my family," says one company owner, "and I always write them birthday notes. Some people have been here for decades, and we all know each other."

An attorney specializing in insurance writes a message to a few employees he works closely with. Sometimes he also gives them flowers or a box of candy.

Here are some suggestions on how to acknowledge a birthday. Because people may not expect to hear from office mates, they're likely to appreciate the effort.

Consider your relationship with the recipient. Some bosses and subordinates have very friendly relationships; others are cordial but correct. A young production manager received a book from her former boss and mentor, who had become a close friend. On the front leaf, the giver wrote:

Dear ————,

> *Life is full of miracles. Follow your dreams and listen to your heart. I wish you much laughter and many miracles in your new birthday year.*
>
> *Yours,*

A partner in a shoe company wrote this note to his office manager:

Dear ————,

> *This place would fall apart without you. Nobody deserves a happy birthday more than you do.*
>
> *Best,*

When in doubt about whether to send a greeting at all—to your boss, for example—it's always appropriate to join in on a group card.

Show appreciation. The vice president of a trade association writes birthday cards in part to stroke staff members' egos. "It's a small office. We can't do a lot of perks, and I want my employees to know they're special." To a secretary he wrote:

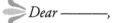

Dear ———,

> *Just want you to know we appreciate what you've done for this office and particularly how you've extended yourself when we needed you.*
>
> *I won't forget how you arranged to set up the meeting while I was traveling and unable to give you complete directions.*
>
> *You are doing a great job. Happy birthday.*
>
> *Best wishes,*

We don't often hear about our good qualities at the office, so people really appreciate praise. "Thoughtful gestures like birthday cards make you feel you're more than just another employee," says a production assistant. "Your colleagues recognize that you have a personal life outside the office."

Individualize your note. Is there a detail in the person's life or your relationship that you can mention? When a client celebrated her fiftieth birthday, a consultant remembered that she had considered taking singing lessons. The consultant wrote:

> Dear ————,
>
>   *Welcome to the wild fifties—full of surprises.*
> *Sing!*
>
>   *Regards,*

Is the person going to a conference in Africa or Eastern Europe? Just "Happy birthday—and have a great trip to Hungary," says, "I'm writing specifically to *you*."

One attorney used humor in this note to a client he'd been trading jokes with for twenty years:

> Dear ————,
>
>   *No one was more surprised than I was to learn that you are only sixty today. I suppose your profligate lifestyle has taken its toll.*
>   *Seriously, though, time has passed too quickly. I wish you many more years of good health and happiness.*
>
>   *Warmly,*

A line like "You're irreplaceable" works well for a group card on which everyone else is writing, "To the only person I know who is older than I am!"

Consider the person's age. Milestones are a time to reflect on what's been achieved and what lies ahead. You can talk about accomplishments and where the person is headed next. Or use a quote like this one, from H. L. Mencken: "The best years are the forties. After fifty a man begins to deteriorate, but in the forties he is at the maximum of his villainy."

You can also mention the accomplishments of other people past a certain age, as in this message to someone at sixty-five:

Dear ——————,

At ninety-four, Brooke Astor retired from philanthropy to travel and write poetry. There is much to look forward to.
Happy birthday.

All the best,

Says a manager, "My colleague was fifty this year, and I've known her for nineteen years. I feel I could call her at three A.M. if my car broke down and she'd come and get me. I debated between saying, 'Who cares if you're fifty?' or rubbing it in." In the end she opted for this message:

Dear ——————,

What would I do without you? I hope our friendship continues stronger than ever. It means a lot to me.
Have a wonderful birthday.

Warmly,

Weddings

"If I'm invited to a wedding of someone from the office, I'm usually pretty close to that person, but it's different in other companies," says a sales director. Sometimes you're invited because it's politically correct or because there are five hundred guests and half the world is on the list. Regardless of the situation, this is the message you want to convey: I recognize this as a momentous event in your life.

Sound enthusiastic. "A wedding is a very big deal," says one executive, "even if it's a second or third marriage. All couples have hopes, dreams, and expectations for the future, and I always try to reflect that in my notes. I usually write, 'The joy of the world to you both.'"

For the remarriage of a longtime client, a tax attorney and his wife gave the couple a gift and this note:

> Dear ———— and ————,
>   We're very excited to share this special day and to see how happy you both look.
>   Congratulations.
>
>   All the best,

When invited to a same-sex wedding, a human resources consultant chose an elegant picture frame and wrote:

> Dear ———— and ————,
>   Congratulations and many happy years together!
>
>   All my good wishes,

Use information the bride and groom have told you. If you know where they're going on their honeymoon, mention it:

> *Dear ———— and ————,*
> *Congratulations and many happy years ahead.*
> *I want to hear all about Fiji when you get back.*
> *Regards,*

Is the bride or groom the child of a colleague or customer? Try to echo what the parent has told you about the couple or the wedding preparations:

> *Dear ———— and ————,*
> *Harry has told us what a devoted couple you*
> *are and how hard you've worked to make this*
> *wedding memorable. We're thrilled to attend.*
> *Congratulations.*
> *Sincerely,*

Talk about the location. Some couples choose to marry at exotic sites these days. Is the wedding being held in a hot air balloon? Or at a zoo? How about "I'll always remember your wedding atop that spectacular mountain"?

One company director was invited to the wedding of two customers who grew herbs for restaurants. The ceremony was held in an open field on their land. The note read:

> *Dear ———— and ————,*
> *How appropriate to hold your wedding on your*
> *beautiful property. I sense much happiness ahead*
> *for you.*
> *Best wishes,*

Tie your note in to your gift. "I don't know how I'd survive without wedding registries," says the executive vice president of a beauty aids company. "The gift you send can affect your reputation in the business world. If the recipient says, 'He sent me this terrible candy dish,' it's damaging. With a registry, you *know* what the couple wants and likes. They fax you a list, you look at it, see the price and what's still available, call them back, and give them your credit card number, and that's it. It's an easy way to make sure the bride and groom get what they really want."

Think about what you want to say on the card beforehand, since you'll have to dictate it to a salesperson over the phone. One stockbroker chose crystal glasses for a couple he knew very well and said:

> *Dear —————— and ——————,*
> *Congratulations and best wishes for a future filled with happiness. Entertain in grand style!*
> *Warmly,*

An assistant buyer chipped in with others to buy a few place settings of a co-worker's silver pattern. On the group card she wrote, "You're a sterling couple. Best of luck on this perfect day!"

Engagements and Showers

If you're invited to an engagement party or bridal shower, your card can refer to the preparations and excitement that lie ahead. Mention looking forward to meeting the partner, if you haven't already. As in the case of a wedding present, you can also talk in your note about your gift, whether it is something formal, such as a crystal bowl, or a household item like cookware or a kitchen gadget.

Some couples prefer more unusual gifts these days. One outdoorsy couple registered at a sporting goods retailer and selected engagement gifts like a ski rack for the car and a water purifier for camping trips. A colleague chose a portable camping stove and wrote this note:

Dear ——— and ———,
  Here's to many fresh-air meals as you hike through life together.

                              Congratulations,

For a bridal shower, you can buy something like a cookbook and refer to using it in the new home or apartment in your note. Give a wedding planner and you can talk about the preparations ahead.

There are times when you're not invited to the wedding or shower, yet still want to acknowledge the event. On these occasions, think about *why* you want to mark it. Is it a good thing to do politically, or do you really *like* the person? The following note fits any situation and works especially well when you don't want to sound too familiar:

Dear ———,
  Just want to add my good wishes to those you've already received.
  Congratulations and much happiness to you and Bill.

                              Best,

If you know the person quite well, you might try something like this:

> Dear ———,
> *I just heard the news about your wedding plans. It's good to know you're settling down. The best of luck to both of you.*
>
> > Regards,

If you know the honeymoon destination, you can also refer to that in your note: "Have a wonderful time in Italy. It sounds like a dream honeymoon."

Births and Adoptions

"I always write notes to clients and contacts who have babies," says a corporate consultant. "They faint with joy because no one else ever writes." She wrote to one:

> Dear ———,
> *This is so wonderful! I'm thrilled to hear the news and that you're both doing well. You're going to be a great mom. Congratulations.*
>
> > Warm regards,

How did the recipient feel? Ecstatic, says the consultant: "She told me, 'Nobody else gave me that kind of compliment. My mother only tells me what I'm doing wrong.'"

Having a child is a time of deep emotion, and new

parents will cherish whatever you write—it's the gesture that counts. However, a personal touch might be especially appreciated. To instantly target your note, use the baby's name, if you know it, and the spouse's, if he or she has been mentioned to you:

Dear ———,
    I'm delighted to hear that Melissa has arrived. Congratulations to you and Harold.

                                            Regards,

An editor always writes something like this: "Jeremy is the luckiest baby. He's got two fabulous parents!" She feels this puts the focus back on mom and dad and makes them feel special.

You might also discuss the baby's name:

Dear ——— and ———,
    Hooray for Harrison. With a first name like that, he's all set to run for president.

                                        Congratulations,

It's also nice to mention the sibling, if there is one: "How wonderful that Elizabeth has a new sister."

Is the mother taking time off for maternity leave? You can say something like, "We're all missing mom" in your note.

Whatever you write, however, take care to avoid stereotypical or sexist statements like "Well, you got a boy at last," implying that boys are valued more than girls.

One corporation sends out E-mail announcements to appropriate employees when a baby is born, saying something like this: "Adam Velez was born today. He weighs eight pounds. His father, Craig, is tired but in good condition. His mother, Barbara, is doing fine."

Should you buy a gift for the new baby? It depends on your relationship with the parents. A senior vice president's rule of thumb is "If I've had several conversations with the parent about the approaching birth, I give a present. I love buying baby gifts."

If you do, too, you can mention the present in your message. The parents of twins received a picture frame with space for two photos. The card read:

> *Dear ———— and ————,*
> *May June and Jeffrey bring you double the joy. I'm sure you've already got plenty of photos to fill this frame.*
>
> *Warmly,*

Did you buy a sweater with a football motif for a nine-pound boy whose parents have described him as a future half-back? Try this note:

> *Dear ———— and ————,*
> *I hear Steven is already planning to be an All-American. This should get him started.*
>
> *Best wishes,*

In many offices, everyone will chip in to buy a going-home outfit for the baby or a gift certificate for a toy or department store. When you sign a group card, you might say, "Welcome to the world. I'm glad all is well."

If you buy a commercial greeting card for adoptive parents, choose it carefully. Avoid cards that specifically refer to either a birth or an adoption. Look instead for terms like "new arrival." You can write:

> *Dear ——— and ———,*
> *What good news! I'm so glad Stacey has arrived and is part of your family. Much joy to all three of you.*
>
> *Best,*

Or how about this:

> *Dear ———,*
> *Welcome to the new addition. Michael couldn't have chosen a better family.*
> *Best of luck to you and Jim and the baby.*
> *Regards,*
>
> *P.S. Bring pictures to the next policy meeting.*

Adoptions can take a long time, and some parents experience several painful disappointments before actually getting a child. In such a case, if the parent has told you about it, you can reflect that in your note:

> *Dear ——— and ———,*
> *I'm thrilled to hear you've finally got Heather. I hear she's really special.*
> *Here's to lots of love and laughter ahead.*
> *Best,*

9

Notes for Christmas and Other Holidays

Holidays provide an opportunity to introduce a personal element to business relationships and to increase your visibility in the eyes of clients and contacts. If you choose your holiday cards with care and add a few handwritten lines to each one, they will serve as goodwill ambassadors that are read, appreciated, and even tacked on the bulletin board.

Christmas

Millions of Americans celebrate Christmas, and it's a tradition for businesses to send cards at this time of year. These cards are vehicles to express appreciation to customers and co-workers and another opportunity to remind people you're around. Here are some ways to help your cards do their job.

Individualize. Some people toss holiday cards away unless they say something personal. One executive writes a line or two on each card, setting aside time to finish the task during the Thanksgiving holiday or even earlier. However hectic your schedule may be, it's still possible to ensure that your greetings make an impression. A handwritten message stands out in a pile of holiday cards, even if it only says, "Here's to a great holiday season for you and Helen."

In some cases—say, if your office is doing a mass mailing of five hundred cards or more—it may not be possible to add a handwritten personal message to each one. But always try to include a handwritten signature. In these situations, you might add a few lines for your A-list of important clients and contacts.

Look at your goal. "I send Christmas cards to customers to say 'Thank you for your business' and to extend good wishes for the New Year," says the owner of a freight company. "The holiday season is a time of reflection, and a little more human contact in a cruel world is a good thing. You hope this will be communicated through the card."

The executive director of a nonprofit sends cards to board members with a simple message:

Dear ———,

Thank you for all your efforts in helping young people grow through your internship programs and for volunteering your services to help make our communities better. Have a wonderful holiday.

Best,

The cards are computer-generated, but the director adds a personal line to each one. To someone at a broadcasting company, he might write, "Congratulations on the purchase of eight more stations. I look forward to working with you to get people involved."

The holidays are also a time to tell employees they're important to you. One director of human resources wrote to a valued assistant:

Dear ———,
   This has been a fantastic year, and it wouldn't have been possible without your backup support. You're one of a kind. Have a great holiday and a happy, healthy New Year.

Warmly,

Choose the card carefully. It *does* matter what the card says. It's wise to avoid overtly religious messages, which is why so many people send "season's greetings" cards. They're safe, since they're appropriate regardless of the recipient's religious affiliation. One office manager orders holiday cards from a museum or the UNICEF catalog and chooses something that mentions peace. Who *doesn't* want world peace?

Consider a New Year's card instead. "I found this 'Happy New Year' card on sale after Christmas," says an executive. "I was feeling guilty because I didn't send out any Christmas cards, and I thought, 'This is perfect.' I've been sending New Year's cards ever since. No one has time to respond to a card at Christmas. It's just one of a million other cards in the mail."

Another executive buys 120 blank cards and writes a note inside each one, saying something like this:

Dear ———,

Thank you for all your business last year. I look forward to working with you in the next.

Best,

Though most people rarely receive thanks for the Christmas cards they send, *she* gets a 50 percent response. "People feel good when they get my card—it's a nice way to end the busy holiday season. And then you can respond back with 'Have you heard about the XYZ merger' or 'I just shipped the Houston order,' and you've got a dialogue going," she says.

If you feel intimidated by blank cards, you can write a line on a printed card, as one literary agent did to an author client:

Dear ———,

Looking forward to more great books with you in the New Year.

Best wishes,

You can also refer to New Year's resolutions or to fresh starts and high hopes, perhaps tying your note in to a future project:

Dear ———,

Here's to success in your search for expanded office space and continued growth in the year ahead.

Happy New Year,

A consultant sends cards that feature quotations from famous people. One year she used this quote:

> Sometimes our light goes out,
> but it is blown again into flame by
> an encounter with another human being.
> Each of us owes deepest thanks to those who
> have rekindled this inner light.
>
> —*Albert Schweitzer*

This short quotation by Harry Truman might work as well:

> "... when people can get excited about
> the ordinary things in life, they live."

You might sign off with something like "Hope all is well and the New Year is a kind one." If you use a different quote every year, it can become a kind of personal signature.

Mention your gifts. Instead of sending cards, one attorney sends a restaurant guide to clients and friends at year's end. "Every time they use it they'll think of us," he says. In the personal note accompanying it, he says, "Eat well in the New Year," or "Hope the New Year brings good health and good eating."

Someone else sends a different inexpensive but useful item every year, such as a miniature tool kit or a travel office supply kit with tape, a ruler, a stapler, and paper clips. The accompanying note reads something like this:

Dear ———,

During the year I always come across interesting items I want to share with friends, and the holiday season gives me an opportunity to do just that. Hope you enjoy the enclosed kit. Happy New Year.

Warmly,

Instead of buying Christmas gifts for accounts, one business owner sends a catalog of $20 or $30 items along with a note asking them to choose their own. To one customer, with whom he shares an interest in stamp collecting, he wrote:

Dear ———,

Please pick something. Happy holiday to you and Mary. Looking forward to seeing you at the February stamp show.

Regards,

He explains, "The person usually doesn't choose it himself; he takes it home to his wife, and she looks at it and they select something together—and all the time they're thinking about my company. Then, when the gift arrives, they think of my company again. That's three hits out of one simple gesture."

Be aware, however, that each corporation has its own culture and rules about giving and receiving gifts. Sometimes it's appropriate to omit the present and send only a personalized card. Many won't accept presents for fear of being accused of bribery or of currying favor. Government regulations forbid others to accept gifts. "Companies that do accept gifts may limit the value to a maximum of $25 or $35," says a protocol expert. "Contact the human resources department and find out about the policy. Check out foreign companies, too. They're not as strict as we are, but it's always wise to know their rules."

Some corporations prefer you to send donations to charity. You can call and ask which one the intended recipient supports, then send an amount such as $25. The person is notified that the donation has been made in his or her name.

When giving gifts to co-workers and subordinates, especially across gender lines, be sensitive and check on company policy. "A bottle of perfume given by a male boss to a female assistant could be misconstrued. In this situation, a better choice might be a gift certificate, so she could pick out her own present," says an etiquette consultant.

At one large corporation, a department head gives each person a $20 gift certificate for a popular store. Her accompanying note focuses on something the recipient did particularly well during the year. It might read, "We're so excited you got the Hong Kong deal. We look forward to watching you really go to town with it next year," or "So glad you're back from maternity leave. The office just wasn't the same without you." Even though a gift certificate is impersonal, it will *feel* personal when it arrives with a message like this.

Says one employee, "I really feel I received a note that couldn't have gone to anyone else. More and more, the busier things get, you really do appreciate the fact that someone took the time to recognize your achievements."

Hanukkah

A celebration of the Festival of Lights, Hanukkah is a joyous Jewish holiday that commemorates the Maccabees' victory over the Syrians in 165 B.C. It takes place before Christmas and lasts eight days. If you wish to send a Hanukkah card to someone, it's nice to add a handwritten personal line or two. Someone wrote this message to a co-worker:

> Dear —————,
>   I'm thinking of you and your family during this holiday season.
>
>   Best wishes,

Or try "Wishing you and your family health and joy in the year ahead." You can make it more personal if you mention the names of family members.

Kwanzaa

Kwanzaa, which means "the first fruits of the harvest," is an African-American holiday that begins on December 26 and, like Hanukkah, lasts for eight days. Linked to African harvest festivals, it focuses on community and family and celebrates seven important principles of life: unity, self-determination, collective work and responsibility, cooperative economics, purpose, creativity, and faith.

Though Kwanzaa wasn't created until 1966, observance of it has grown tremendously. Special foods, gifts, dinners, and parties are associated with it. Candles are lit.

If you are sure the person celebrates Kwanzaa and you wish to send a Kwanzaa card, try adding a message:

Dear ———,
   I know this is a special occasion and wish you
   and your family a joyous Kwanzaa celebration.
                                                    Warmly,

Other Holidays

As the holiday season becomes increasingly multicultural, it's important to recognize the many diverse elements. A card is one way to show you're aware of what others celebrate.

Three Kings Day is a Latino religious celebration that takes place on January 6. It celebrates the day the Magi paid homage to the infant Jesus in the manger. In Puerto Rico and other Latin cultures, it can be a more important holiday than Christmas, and gifts are given. If you wish to acknowledge it to an employee or associate, add a few words to the holiday card you send, as in "Merry Christmas (or Happy New Year) and a joyous Three Kings Day."

Chinese New Year usually falls between January 19 and February 20. There are fireworks and dragon dancer parades, and gifts are exchanged. You can buy cards in English and Chinese in Chinatown bookstores, stationery stores, and UNICEF gift shops in New York and other big cities.

One nice thing to do is find out the Chinese zodiac symbol for that year. One year might be the year of the snake, the symbol of wisdom, for example. Then you can refer to that symbol in your note:

Dear —————,
   I understand this is the year of the ox, the symbol of the harvest, and that it's a good year. Have a wonderful celebration.

Sincerely,

Eid is a Muslim holiday that stands out as a celebration. It's the day after the last day of Ramadan, a month of fasting and atonement. The exact date varies every year. Eid is a feast day on which presents are exchanged. Cards in English and Arabic are available in ethnic and UNICEF stores. You can add something like "Wishing you a wonderful holiday celebration."

Every country also has its own national holidays. The national holiday for Poland, for example, is May 3. If you wish to find out more about other countries' holidays, contact the appropriate embassy in Washington, D.C., or seek out the information center or chamber of commerce for the specific nationality or group. You can find listings of these organizations in the phone book in many large cities.

10

Get-Well Notes

When people are sick or incapacitated, especially if they are hospitalized, they feel anxious and vulnerable. They want to hear from others. They particularly appreciate get-well notes from business associates because they know, in most cases, that you didn't *have* to write; you *chose* to write. Your note sends the message "I care. I'm concerned about you." Some recipients are so touched that they will vividly remember your gesture even years later.

What can you write? It depends on your relationship and the nature of the illness or injury.

When a magazine promotion manager stepped off a curb and broke her foot during her pregnancy, she was deluged with cards and notes from co-workers. Quips like "You obviously flunked out of ballet school" kept her chuckling through a difficult time.

It's easy to write a funny message in situations such as this one. Humor works here because the person will soon be hobbling around the office and recuperating.

It's a lot tougher to write when an illness is life-threatening or when recovery is unlikely or uncertain. Yet people do want to be remembered. A personalized card or note is good medicine, and sending one is a human thing to do. Since cards and notes are often kept and displayed, it can be good business as well.

The exact message will depend on how well you know the person and how forthcoming the patient is with information about his or her condition. There are boundaries when dealing with illness, and it's important not to cross them, especially in business relationships. Individual companies and departments also have different styles; there can be great intimacy at work in some cases, strict formality in others. Only you know the atmosphere of your office and the proper approach to take.

When in doubt, the best policy is a group card, sent with or without flowers, which everyone signs. It keeps the focus off any single person. If the patient is a customer, you can send flowers on behalf of the company and write a note on the card: "The staff at Smith Ltd. wishes you a speedy recovery."

What Do You Want to Say?

Diagnosis and prognosis count. Humor is welcome when the situation is right, but be sure you know what's going on. You'll write differently to a heart patient than to someone having hemorrhoid surgery.

When the wife of a client and close personal friend had a hip replacement, a consultant sent an orchid plant to the hospital. The card, which referred to the fact that *both* the patient and the consultant had been limping recently, read, "Dear ———, From one gimp to another—here's to a smooth recovery. Best."

You can tie your note in to a personal interest or

habit of the patient. Take the case of a manager who spent hours on his knees planting tulips—and wound up with a blood clot in one leg. A colleague sent flowers and wrote, "To a fellow *former* gardener, from your friend ———." Someone else wrote, "When did you decide you had such a green thumb?"

Refer to your connection to the person. A sportswear manufacturer who was hospitalized for gall bladder surgery received a group card from his office staff with handwritten messages like this: "Dear Mr. ———, Please hurry back. We miss your E-mail." His partner wrote, "I miss the smell of your cigars! Get well fast!" If you write an individual note, you can also mention some office gossip that may be of interest, if that seems appropriate.

Some people feel so tongue-tied in a very serious situation that they may be tempted not to write at all. Remember that you don't have to write poetry. Says an executive who was critically injured in an accident, "I just wanted to hear 'I'm thinking of you.'" Those four words are very powerful. The whole idea is to make a human connection, and you *can* do it with that one line. "We miss you" and "You're on my mind" both say something meaningful, too.

In some cases, a note is hard to write because of the sensitive nature of the surgery or because you can't relate to it. Just keep in mind that you don't *have* to relate to it. Treat it like any surgery. A male partner in a consulting firm wrote this note to a female office manager recovering from a hysterectomy:

Dear ———,

> *Hope you're doing well. Please take care of*
> *yourself and get all the rest you need. I'm eager to*
> *see you back at your desk soon. The place just isn't*
> *the same without you.*
>
> Best,

A lobbyist will never forget the note he received while recuperating from a coronary bypass. It consisted of two sentences, written by a deputy commissioner in the federal government—someone he dealt with regularly:

Dear ———,

> *Get back here so I can pick on you again! Hope*
> *all is going well.*
>
> Best,

When a stockbroker suffered a heart attack on an airplane while returning home from a meeting, a colleague who had attended the same meeting wrote:

Dear ———,

> *I was shocked to hear about what happened on*
> *your trip home. I wish you a smooth recovery.*
> *All of your friends are thinking of you.*
>
> Sincerely,

When the diagnosis is cancer, it's critical to be sensitive. Don't write at all unless the person has personally told you about it. People often consider it a very private matter, and they may fear that word will get out and affect their career.

If someone *has* told you of the diagnosis and you want to write, be positive. Focus on showing the ways in which that person is needed. Says a business owner, "One employee of forty years died of cancer last year after a long illness. We had shared an office for a long time. I called her every day when she was sick, and I'd write to her, 'Without you, this place is a bad dream.' I wanted to make her feel special."

Is a friend and associate undergoing radiation therapy? You might try something like "I hope the treatments go fast."

An administrator wrote this note to the wife of a close colleague who had four months to live:

> *Dear* ———,
>
> *I can't imagine how stressful this must be for you. If there's anything I can do, like driving Joe to treatment or to the doctor, let me know.*
>
> *Best regards,*

Another daunting task is writing to someone whose child is very ill. Yet a buyer for a specialty retailer received many notes from associates as her son lay near death from a rare form of leukemia. Her favorite came from a co-worker who knew she was religious:

> *Dear* ———,
>
> *This must be a nightmare. But I am confident that Adam will get through this. Have faith in God and don't give up.*
>
> *I am praying for both of you.*
>
> *Warmly,*

"I thought I was going to lose my son," says the buyer, "and I needed to hear something encouraging. You want to know there's a chance, and these words gave me strength. Hundreds of people were praying for him." Her son's leukemia is now in remission.

If you don't know whether or not the person is religious, or if you know he or she definitely is not, you can still say, if you wish, "Amy is in my prayers." People appreciate the support at a time like this. You can add a simple, "Please know that I am thinking of both of you."

Or you can take another approach, such as this note written to a client by an account executive for a public relations firm:

Dear ————,

I just heard about Karen. You've mentioned her so often I feel I know her.

If there is any way I can help, please let me know.

Sincerely,

Don't offer to help in a case like this, however, unless you really intend to do so and have something practical to offer.

What do you write to a hospitalized AIDS patient? You might say something like this:

Dear ————,

You have friends who care, and you are in our thoughts. If we can be of help, please let us know.

Sincerely,

People want to know that they haven't been forgotten.

There are other situations, too, where the best thing to do is to say what you feel and write from your heart. To a subordinate who was diagnosed with ALS (Lou Gehrig's disease), one sales manager wrote:

Dear ——————,

Nobody deserves this, but you especially don't. For years you have been the sunshine of the sales department, and all of us miss you. Know that we and so many others here are thinking of you and that we care.

All the best,

11

Condolence Notes

When my mother died, I got very personal notes
from people I work and do business with. You
could tell they came from the heart, and I was so
appreciative that they made the effort. It's not so
much what you say, but the fact that you were
thinking of the person.

—Recording executive

For most of us, the hardest thing to write is a condolence note. We see the obituary or hear the news through the office grapevine, and we feel at a loss for words. Yet there is much you can say in just a few sentences.

The point of a condolence note is to express sympathy and to acknowledge the recipient's loss. Your note should be sincere and handwritten; this is *not* the time for E-mail. If you send a printed condolence card, avoid anything religious, and add a line or two of your own.

Whatever you write, keep it very brief unless you are extremely close to the recipient or the person who has died. These guidelines will help.

Personalize. Say something specific, even if you're writing to someone you've never met, such as the widow of a colleague. A remark like "With deepest sympathy on the loss of your loved one" is very general and could apply to anyone. At least mention *who* has died, as in "on the loss of your *sister*." A little detail like that matters. If you wish, you can add, "You are in our thoughts," which is what people want and need to hear.

One vice president wrote this thoughtful note to an associate:

> Dear ————,
>
> I am so sorry to hear of your mother's death. I know this is a difficult time. If there is anything we can do to help, please let us know.
>
> Sincerely,

An office manager wrote to her boss's wife:

> Dear Mrs. ————,
>
> I was so sorry to hear about your father's death. There is so little anyone can say at a time like this. I do want you to know that you are in my prayers.
>
> Sincerely,

If you attended the funeral, you can refer to the service. An executive assistant had helped with some last-minute arrangements, and was able to draw on that in a note to her supervisor's family:

Dear ———,

The service for your father was a beautiful one.
I'm glad I was able to help the family a little.
Please accept my sincere sympathy for your loss.
Sincerely,

If you knew the deceased personally, talk about him or her. A condolence note is also a way to memorialize someone who has died. The family wants to know the person made an impact on others and won't be forgotten. A banker wrote to the widow of his former boss:

Dear ———,

John made a tremendous difference in my life.
I feel grateful to him for many reasons. When I
was changing careers, he was the first person in
banking who really listened to what I had to say.
He paid attention. He had confidence in me,
which gave me confidence.

John talked of you and your sons so often over
the years. I want you to know that I'm thinking
of you. If there is any way at all that I can be of
help, please let me know.

Sincerely,

Says the banker, "I really meant it. I wrote because I remember how I felt when my father died. It was right after I got my degree, and the thing that helped me most was going to the church and finding it packed. It was a way for strangers to say to me, 'We loved him too.' I wanted to do the same for someone else."

119

An accountant wrote to the widow of one of his colleagues from another company:

Dear ———,

I was shocked and saddened to learn of Leonard's passing. He was truly one of the leaders in the industry.

Over the many years I knew him, nothing gave me greater pleasure than to discuss with him some esoteric point in the tax code. He always kept me on my toes, and I will miss him.

Please convey my condolences to your family.

Sincerely,

When a client and friend lost his only brother, a marketing consultant talked about a memory:

Dear ———,

I can't believe that Greg is gone. I know what a blow this is to you.

I remember meeting him for the first time at dinner at Marco's a few years ago. We talked about his trade show in Atlanta.

Things change too fast.

Take care of yourself and remember I'm always here.

Sincerely,

Mention a personality trait. An attorney sent a fruit basket to an old friend and colleague whose father had died. The attorney had known the father for years and wrote on the gift card:

Dear ———,

　Please accept my sincere condolences. In all of my dealings with Larry, he was unfailingly kind and generous.

Sincerely,

When a stationer he had dealt with for many years died, a business owner wrote to the widow:

Dear ———,

　I have never met you, but I've known Arthur for many years and want you to know how sad I feel to hear of his death.

　He was a good businessman and a supplier I could always depend on; he was also a fine person. I especially enjoyed his sense of humor. I always knew when he had a new joke—he'd call me right away.

　His death is a loss for everyone.

Sincerely,

Sometimes a death comes from out of the blue. When her former secretary died from complications of the flu, a manager wrote to the woman's daughter:

Dear ———,

　It was such a shock to hear about Sarah's death. I can't tell you how sorry I am. She was a dynamo and the most loyal, dependable person I've ever worked with. I don't know what I would have done without her wonderful support.

　I grieve with you.

Sincerely,

Says the writer, "The daughter wrote back, telling me how pleased her mother would have been to know the warm regard I had for her. I answered with a note that said, 'She knew.'"

Consider the circumstances. When a client's wife died after a long illness, an attorney wrote to him:

> *Dear ———,*
>
> *It was almost two years ago that you told me Emily was ill. Between then and now, we have spoken many times about her condition and your feelings.*
>
> *She was lucky to have you. Your care and understanding throughout the illness were brave, wonderful things. I hope you can take comfort in that and in all the years the two of you spent together.*
>
> *She leaves behind a wonderful family, to whom I send my profound sympathy.*
>
> *Warmly,*

When a close colleague died of cancer, a director of communications wrote to the widow:

> *Dear ———,*
>
> *Bill's death still isn't real to me. I see him sitting in your living room the last time we visited, looking better than I expected and trying to figure out his next move. I don't know what we will do without him.*
>
> *I am so sorry for your loss. Know that we are all thinking of you.*
>
> *Warmly,*

An AIDS death is especially difficult to write about because the family may not acknowledge the actual cause. In a situation where they did, a friend wrote:

Dear ———,

A message on the AIDS quilt says, 'Don't forget me.' Jeff will not be forgotten—by me or by anyone else who knew him well. My husband, Frank, joins me in sending sympathy to you and your family.

Warmly,

If the family does not acknowledge the AIDS connection, do not mention it and treat your note as you would a note for any difficult death. It's always appropriate to talk about a memory.

Be honest about how you feel. Instead of hiding genuine feelings, *use* them, especially when tragedy strikes. Did a colleague die in a commuter plane crash? You can say, "I feel shell-shocked. This is something you read about in the papers. It doesn't happen to people you know. I can't believe Jerry won't be sitting at his desk tomorrow morning."

What could surpass the pain of the death of a child? Are you feeling as if you don't know what to say to the parent? Write it: "This is so terrible. I don't know what to say." That is one of the most meaningful things you can write. "I can't imagine what you are going through" is another powerful line for tragic situations.

An architect wrote this note to a client whose son had died:

> *Dear ———,*
>
> *In my religion there is an expression which, loosely translated, says, "May our children outlive us." The loss of a child is more than any of us can bear.*
>
> *As a parent myself, I can't conceive of the grief that you and your family must feel. My thoughts are with you all.*
>
> *Sincerely,*

An executive wrote this note to someone whose daughter was murdered:

> *Dear ———,*
>
> *I've been thinking of you ever since the funeral and want you to know you're in the thoughts of everyone at the office. Jennifer's death is such a tragic loss.*
>
> *No one can presume to know what you must be going through.*
>
> *Sincerely,*

No one *can* presume to know, which is why it's important never to say "I know how you feel." Do not talk at length about how you felt when your mother died. Someone else may feel very differently. The focus should be on the bereaved or the deceased, not on you.

Beware, too, of saying things like, "I hope you will find some comfort in memories of good times"— unless you know for a fact that there *were* good times. Relationships can be very troubled. Do not assume anything about anybody.

Acknowledgments of Condolences

Acknowledgments are in order when people send notes, cards with a personalized message, donations to charity, or baskets of fruit or food. Add a handwritten line or two to a printed acknowledgement card or write a brief note. "Writing can actually be a catharsis," says an etiquette expert. One option:

> Dear —————,
>   Your contribution to Smithtown Hospital in memory of William meant a lot to me. Thank you for your generosity and thoughtfulness.
>   Sincerely,

An administrator wrote this note to a close colleague:

> Dear —————,
>   Thank you for your kind words and sympathy at a very difficult time. Your note provided a great deal of comfort, especially your recollection of Tim. It's nice to know he made an impact on others. I appreciate your thoughtfulness.
>   Sincerely,

Or try this:

> Dear —————,
>   It takes an occasion like this to really realize how much friends mean. Your gift of food was especially thoughtful. Thanks from us all.
>   Regards,

12

Thank-You Notes

All the etiquette books say you should write
thank-you notes for everything—even when
someone gives you tickets to a concert or takes
you out to dinner. But is it really necessary?

—*Financial writer*

Whether a thank-you note is necessary isn't the issue—smart business *is*. Etiquette is the ultimate business tool. Practicing it will help you make a good impression so that you will stand out in a sea of competitors. Thank-you notes are also one more opportunity to put your name in front of people and cement relationships in and out of your company.

General Strategies

It makes sense to write thank-you notes because not everyone does. Short ones work best. "Most of mine are two sentences because no one is going to read anything longer," says a tax consultant. Try these tips for effective notes:

Write promptly. "Many executives think it's a pain to write a thank-you," says an etiquette expert, "but it's easy enough to do it immediately and get it over with. Before you go to lunch, put a correspondence card on your desk and address the envelope. Then all you have to do when you return is write, "Thank you for a great lunch. I enjoyed seeing you, and I look forward to discussing the project with you at greater length."

Sound sincere and enthusiastic. "What separates a good note from an average one is an expression of genuine appreciation for a gift or a favor," says a sales manager.

Do you really love the gift? Did you enjoy the dinner or the show? Say so:

> Dear ———,
>
> What an exciting evening! I love the ballet, and Swan Lake was magical.
> Thanks so much for inviting me.
>
> > Best,

People want to know they've made you happy, and, yes, there is an element of flattery here.

Describe the gift or experience. Specifically mention how an object looks and how you will use it:

> Dear ———,
>
> The marble bookends are handsome and blend right in with the cabinets in my new office. They're just what I needed.
> Thank you for your thoughtfulness.
>
> > Best regards,

When a gift arrived from an appreciative client, a career counselor wrote:

> Dear ————,
>
> The brown leather day planner is beautiful, and your timing is perfect. It's November and I'm ready to throw out my old one, which isn't nearly as good-looking.
>
> Thank you so much. It's been a pleasure to work with you.
>
> Sincerely,

It's especially nice to describe a gift basket. The sender probably ordered it by phone and doesn't know what it looks like or exactly what it contains. Someone wrote this thank-you note:

> Dear ————,
>
> The delicacies in the exquisite Christmas basket you sent to the office were devoured as soon as the paper was off. The basket looked so festive, wrapped in red and green, and it was filled with delicious smoked salmon, cheeses, fruits, and cookies.
>
> Thank you for being so thoughtful. I hope you had the happiest of holidays.
>
> Warm regards,

A real estate agent who always receives citrus fruit from a longtime client at Christmas wrote this note one year:

> Dear ————,
>
> This is such a nice tradition. We enjoy the grapefruits and oranges so much.

128

Thank you for thinking of us year after year.
Happy holidays.

All the best,

Remember small gestures. Thank-yous for thoughtful little gifts can provide you with a chance to connect. Many businesspeople share a fondness for cigars. When a friend sent a few king-sized samples, a stockbroker wrote:

Dear ———,

As I write this, I'm smoking one of the cigars you brought back from your trip. It will take me two weeks. Thanks for remembering me.

Regards,

An accountant wrote this thank-you note:

Dear ———,

I am about to leave for a partner retreat (I think it should be called an advance), and instead of a toothbrush I packed the cigars you sent.

You're a good guy, and I look forward to many good times together. Can I help with your recruitment of a controller and an office manager?
Thanks.

Sincerely,

While on a business trip, a client introduced an attorney to a new garnish for martinis. The lawyer liked it so much that the client sent him a jar, which prompted this note:

> *Dear ———,*
>
> *You have proven once again that New Orleans is the center of the universe and that all good things emanate from there. The tomolives arrived just in time for Thanksgiving, and I can't wait to see what my family thinks of them.*
>
> *Thanks for remembering.*
>
> > *Best,*

Say that you had a good time. Did you have dinner at the boss's home? How about this thank-you:

> *Dear ——— and ———,*
>
> *Many thanks for inviting us to your home last Saturday. Dinner was delicious, particularly that irresistible chocolate torte.*
>
> *We had a wonderful time.*
>
> > *Sincerely,*

When you write a thank-you note after you've been invited somewhere, you can also talk about the ambience, the good conversation, and the other guests. If you wish, you can add something like "The evening ended much too soon." We all want to hear that we're successful hosts.

When an attorney gave a business friend legal advice without charge, the recipient showed appreciation by hosting a gala evening out. The attorney wrote:

> *Dear ———,*
>
> *It was a great night, seeing Bobby Short at the Carlyle. You don't get quality entertainment like that anymore—a combination of sophistication,*

nostalgia, and exuberance—and the food wasn't
bad, either!

We'd like to see Eartha Kitt next, so please try
to stay in trouble. Thanks for an evening we
won't soon forget.

Best,

After attending the fiftieth birthday party of a business associate in the South of France, a company owner wrote:

Dear ———,

Your birthday was unforgettable. Partying on
top of the world in a beautiful restaurant over-
looking the Mediterranean was like a fantasy
come true.

We thank you for a spectacular night.

Regards,

P.S. Enclosed are some photos we took at the party.

Did a broadcasting executive invite you to sit in his company box at a sporting event? How about this note:

Dear ———,

TV is fine, but nothing compares to the real
thing. The match was sensational. Thanks for a
great day.

Best regards,

Why should you write if *you're* the customer? Because you will benefit from maintaining good relationships with your advertising salesman, printer, accountant, insurance agent, and others who provide products or services you need. These people can make your business run smoothly, find ways to save you money, provide information, and sometimes even serve as matchmakers for joint ventures or for jobs.

Did your stationery supplier send you tickets to a sold-out show? How about this thank-you:

Dear ————,

> *Betsy and I loved the show. We don't know how you managed to get the hottest tickets in town, but we're certainly glad you did.*
> *Thanks for a great evening.*

> > *Best,*

Keep negatives to yourself. The idea is to make others feel good. If the gift is useless, tasteless, or a duplicate of something you already have, focus instead on the giver. Talk about a positive quality, such as generosity or imagination. What if the flowers are dead on arrival or the oranges are overripe and inedible? "I'd never bring it to the sender's attention," says an etiquette expert. "Criticism makes people feel bad. Acknowledge the thought behind the gift, and then forget it."

If a valued client sends you a gift box of filets mignons —and you don't eat meat—try something like this:

Dear ————,

> *How nice of you to send the steaks. They look delicious.*
> *You're as thoughtful as ever. Thanks for remembering me—again.*

> > *Regards,*

Wedding Gifts

Wedding-gift thank-yous are a unique challenge because you inevitably face a pile of them. Nevertheless, there's no excuse for waiting months to thank anyone, and it's particularly unwise to delay writing to someone with whom you have a business relationship. Tardiness leaves the sender wondering whether you ever received the gift. Many couples divide the task: she writes to her connections; he writes to his.

Your thank-you note should not sound like a form letter with the blanks filled in. Instead, convey the message, "*Your* gift was special." People often buy expensive presents for weddings and deserve extra attention.

One executive and his wife solved the time problem by taking thank-you cards along on their Caribbean honeymoon. While they sat and sunned, they wrote notes together, using the locale to add interest:

Dear ———,

    As we sit by the pool in Puerto Rico, we just had to thank you for the elegant Wedgwood serving platter. It will be a special part of our holiday dinners and celebrations in the years to come.

                                  Regards,

A hotel manager wrote:

Dear ———,

    Your silver frame already contains our wedding picture. It looks wonderful sitting on the buffet. It meant a lot to us to celebrate with you.

                                  Regards,

Baby Gifts

"When my first son was born," says an executive, "one of our managers sent us a silver spoon with the baby's monogram. It was a lovely gift, and I tried to tell her how much it meant to us, to focus on our feelings and not just her thoughtfulness." He wrote:

Dear ———,

   Now I can say that Zachary was born with a silver spoon in his mouth. This is something we will treasure. Whenever we look at it in years to come, we'll also think of your kindness.
   Thanks so much.

Regards,

The recipient, touched by the note, told him, "I was expecting a note along the lines of 'Thanks for the great spoon. We really like it a lot,' but yours meant so much more and made me feel that my gift was truly appreciated."

If the gift is clothing, describe how the baby looks in it. If it's a toy, show how it's being used:

Dear ———,

   Amy can't take her eyes off the crib mobile. What a great idea! Thanks for your thoughtfulness.

Regards,

Thank-Yous for Group Gifts

Some companies or departments give group gifts for weddings, showers, births, adoptions, and retirements. If you receive a gift from four people or fewer, write an individual note of thanks to each one, suggests an etiquette consultant. If the gift is from five or more people, write one note that can be posted on the bulletin board for all to see.

When a speaker who runs seminars received a Christmas gift from ten people at a seminar company, she wrote:

> To the faculty,
> What a thoughtful thing to do. I really appreciate the laser pointer. It will definitely come in handy.
> I look forward to working with all of you next year.
>
> Best regards,

An assistant vice president of an automobile accessories company wrote this thank-you note for a group wedding gift:

> To everyone in the Human Resources Department,
> The Tiffany clock is magnificent. I was thrilled when I opened the elegant box and saw it. Now I can't be late anymore!
> I'll never forget your beautiful gift and your thoughtfulness. You really made me feel special.
>
> Sincerely,

A financial analyst wrote this thank-you note for a retirement gift:

> *To my colleagues in accounting,*
> *It isn't easy to leave Barker and Sons after twenty-five years, especially when I am fortunate enough to have worked with friends like you.*
> *Your taste in watches is superb. I'll be wearing mine every day and thinking of all of you. Thank you for a wonderful gift and great memories.*
> *Regards,*

If there's a death in your family and your co-workers chip in to send flowers to the funeral home, you might write something like this:

> *To my friends at TNR, Inc.,*
> *Thank you for sending the beautiful flowers. My husband's death has been really hard, and it helps to know that others care.*
> *I'll always remember your thoughtfulness.*
> *Sincerely,*

Part Four

Power Tools

13

Electronic Notes

E-mail and faxes have changed our lives at work, making communication faster, easier, and more casual than ever before. The benefits are enormous, but these modern means of communication are not without limitations and rules. When you know your way around them, it's easier to maximize productivity *and* make a positive impression.

E-Mail

An ideal vehicle for quick notes, E-mail is informal and efficient. "It cuts out so much back-and-forth time," says an executive. "If you just had lunch with someone and want your sales manager to know the person will call her, you E-mail a note. You don't have to call, find she's out, leave a message, and have her get back to you when *you're* out. She'll read your note when she gets there, and the task is accomplished."

E-mail can also provide access to people you might not otherwise reach. "A lot of higher-ups answer their own E-mail," says a business communications expert. "If you're the president of a professional organization looking for a speaker and you phone the head of a company, a secretary will filter the call. But if you use E-mail, you might get a response. Of course, you have to be diplomatic. Be polite and quick, and send your message only once."

E-mail is also a nonintrusive way to communicate; people can reply to their mail at their convenience. It allows you to stay in touch internationally, too, and to disseminate news to many people in your organization. Says one boss, "E-mail increases communication with employees. You just type a message, push a button, and it's sent. You don't have to distribute a million different pieces of paper." Some companies that want to cut back on paper use *expect* employees to communicate by E-mail.

Just because E-mail is convenient and informal, however, you shouldn't assume that rules don't apply. Here's what you need to know about electronic etiquette:

Be brief. E-mail is best used for a short message, as in "Must know by 10:00 A.M. tomorrow: how many cases of samples do we need for the Simon Company introduction?" In one office, it's an unwritten rule that the message should fit on the screen without scrolling.

Stick to one topic. Pare down your message and get to the point fast: "I think we should hire this candidate. Yes?" When you fill in the subject line, be as specific as possible: "Get approval on annual report." This line can flag attention and signal someone to read your message before others.

Be correct. What you present to the business world through ordinary correspondence applies to electronic communication as well. There's a tendency to get sloppy with E-mail and forget that it's a document that can affect your image. Don't use it as an excuse to forget about correct spelling and grammar or to be overly familiar with someone. In one case, a potential employer asked for copies of a job candidate's E-mail to see how the person structured her thoughts.

Experts recommend using a salutation, along with a closing. Though "Dear ———" isn't *required*, it does personalize your E-mail. Says one on-line service executive, "I feel that 'Sincerely' sounds too formal in E-mail, so I sign off with 'Regards' or 'Best.'" When you want a more casual tone, begin with the person's name, as in, "Joe, the meeting is at two o'clock." Save "Hi" for your friends; it's too informal for business communication, and it annoys some people.

Protect your privacy. Don't say anything in E-mail that you wouldn't say in written correspondence. You don't know who might see it. Management can search E-mail, and it has been used as evidence in court proceedings. Remember also that the recipient can forward your E-mail to other people without your knowledge or your permission.

Reread your memo before you send it. Are you sure your message is clear? Avoid abbreviations such as BTW (by the way) and IMO (in my opinion). They are inappropriate in business E-mail, and many people don't know what they stand for.

Read messages you *receive* carefully before you reply, too. In one case, someone saw a notice on a professional organization's electronic bulletin board that said, "William Harris's mother died. Fax or phone."

Thinking it inappropriate to fax, the person mailed a condolence note. A few days later the recipient called to say, "It was a lovely note—but my mother died in 1973." The sender mentioned the electronic notice. Replied the caller, "It didn't say my mother died. It said my *modem* died." So much for quick scans of the screen.

Don't use E-mail to criticize or to express anger. Typed, handwritten, or printed correspondence slows you down and gives you time to cool off and reconsider. You have to print or write the message, address the envelope, and put it into the mail. If you send a quick E-mail, you may be sorry the next morning.

Don't type an entire message in capital letters, either. It's considered rude—the equivalent of shouting at someone—and it's hard to read.

Avoid unnecessary messages. "Do you know how many E-mail messages I *have* to deal with every day? Just drop me a note; don't send me E-mail!" says a marketing director. Remember, too, that nothing will replace talking face-to-face with colleagues, subordinates, and your boss. If you overdo E-mail and send it for everything, you can dilute its impact. Here's a general guideline: if they E-mail you, you can E-mail your reply.

Is E-Mail Appropriate for This Message?

A corporate consultant normally prefers to speak to clients by phone or face-to-face because the contact is more personal. But she uses E-mail in select situations, such as to mention something she forgot to say earlier.

Dear ———,

When I spoke to you I forgot to mention that Knowles & Co. is interested in using my services and wants a reference. Because I've worked with you for five years, I'd like to give your name. Please let me know if that's okay.

Sincerely,

She used E-mail to contact a university professor whose research she wanted to mention in her new book. Since she had the professor's E-mail address but not his phone number, she wrote:

Dear ———,

I'm writing a book about business relationships and would like to talk to you about your article, which was published in the last issue of the Journal of Social and Personal Relationships. *Can we arrange a phone interview? I look forward to hearing from you.*

Sincerely,

E-mail does not have the weight of importance of a handwritten note. But it can be useful in certain casual situations—for example, when you want to say a quick "Thank you for sending that article" or "Good work." When and whether you use it will depend on the situation and on your relationship with the recipient. An etiquette expert says, "I send some season's greetings notes internationally by E-mail, because that has been our method of communication all along. But I send handwritten cards and notes to domestic clients."

Promotions are often publicized throughout a company via E-mail. If you've received an E-mail notice that a co-worker has been promoted or has won an award, you might want to E-mail a quick note of congratulations to her. A manager E-mailed this note to a colleague who was named head of a division:

Dear ——,

Congratulations. I heard you were just promoted to division manager. Please say hello to Janet and the girls.

Regards,

E-mail can bring good wishes that might not ordinarily be expressed. To the same colleague who received a promotion, a senior executive wrote, "I think this is great. Your contributions have been outstanding. What a wonderful way for the company to recognize you."

The executive admits, "I know that E-mail is not as personal as a handwritten note. My concern was that if I passed up the opportunity to use E-mail, I'd never get around to writing the note."

One thing we don't do enough of is send thank-yous to co-workers who have helped us. This E-mail message went to an entire department that. had worked hard on an event: "Many thanks for assisting in promoting the seminar, especially to those on the front lines who answered questions. Special thanks to Betty and Dick, who were on the planning committee and did a great job. Also, thanks to the presenters, whose quality information and clever presentation styles made the event so successful."

The president of a professional organization sent this E-mail message to committee heads:

To: New Committee Heads
From: Lamar Dunham

Many thanks to all of you—new committee heads and those of you who have reenlisted—for agreeing to lead one of our important committees for this year.

Your first chore is to organize your committee and have its members in place. The list of members needs to go to Rita Harrigan by March 9.

It is always our best people who agree to do this kind of work, and so I am looking forward to a great year.

E-mail is so new that the rules are still evolving. Often you will have to rely on common sense and good judgment. "I think it's okay to broadcast a thank-you on E-mail when you get taken out to lunch by eight people from the office," says an executive. "But if you receive a wedding gift from someone, you should take

145

the time to compose an individual handwritten note to the person."

It is *never* acceptable to send a condolence via E-mail. It is also inappropriate to resign or to fire someone that way.

Faxes

Faxes are ideal for sending documents, signed correspondence on letterhead, and other materials fast. People are still thinking through the rules as technology continues to evolve.

No matter how or what you fax, send along a cover sheet with your name and your fax and phone numbers. Describe the nature of the material you're sending so the recipient will know what this is about. Some people write on the cover sheet, "Original will follow," and then send the original by mail.

Keep the fax as brief as possible and do not send unsolicited faxes. They can be an unwelcome intrusion and may tie up a machine. They are also a waste of paper and can mean that the machine will have to be reloaded. You don't want the recipient to wind up mad at you. "Someone once sent me a twenty-page fax I didn't need. I was *not* happy," says a communications consultant.

Remember that faxes, like E-mail, are not private communications. Anyone can pass by and read them, and they can get lost en route to the intended recipient.

14

Stationery and Pens

A good business note is about more than just words. Since presentation counts, remember that your stationery and pen also make an important statement. They represent you and are part of your image. Here's how to make a good impression.

Stationery

Are you a physician or an investment banker who wants to project a conservative, traditional image—or a fashion editor who wants something a little more cutting-edge? Are you an executive vice president or an administrative assistant? The perfect stationery for a graphic designer is different from what suits a CPA.

What's appropriate depends not only on your position and your business but also on the audience and purpose of the note. Many people don't need the finest stationery for everyday correspondence or for invoices and internal memos. But good stationery makes sense when writing to important customers and contacts.

Essentials

Business stationery can be either formal or more casual, and it's nice to have options for a range of situations. If you work for someone else, you may want to supplement company-issued stationery with your own correspondence cards. Says an etiquette authority, "Your office may give you stationery, but sometimes you want to write on a more personal level. We all have our own style. You may just use letterhead and envelopes, or you can adopt a more casual tone for certain occasions."

Here are some suggestions for business stationery, though you may not need to use all of them.

Company letterhead. This is the standard 8½- by 11-inch size for business letters. Choose white or ecru paper with black or dark blue ink if you're in a conservative field like insurance, banking, accounting, law, architecture, or medicine. Black ink on gray stock is a third alternative. If your company has a logo, it might appear on the letterhead as well.

A wholesale florist, on the other hand, would probably want something less conservative. And an interior designer might choose a nontraditional yet elegant look using bright-colored ink. An entertainment executive might select something very modern, such as marbled paper, for his company.

"Your stationery represents *you*," says a fine stationer. "If it's got big script letters in purple ink and a flashy gold border, my first thought would be 'This person is fun.' A fashion photographer might want to convey that impression."

Use letterhead when you intend to use a formal tone—for example, in a pat-on-the-back or a happy birthday note to a subordinate, for a businesslike thank-you note for a referral, or for a formal note of congratulations on a promotion. You might also use letterhead to say thank you for a Christmas gift when the sender is someone you don't know, such as the management of your office building. It's considered entirely appropriate to send handwritten notes on any business stationery, including letterhead.

Monarch letterhead. The trend to shorter correspondence has increased the popularity of monarch- and smaller-size sheets. Intended for business use, business-personal use, and more informal occasions, monarch letterhead is 7¼ by 10½ inches. It's an option for thank-you notes and staying-in-touch notes.

"A monarch-size note is nice as a follow-up when you've established a relationship with a networking contact," says a consultant. "You can write by hand and say, 'Thanks for seeing me the other day. Here's a copy of my résumé, as you requested.'"

Correspondence card. This is another choice for business and business-social occasions. It is ideal for handwritten thank-you notes, condolences, and congratulations mainly because you can fit only four or five lines on it. Normally your name appears at the top of the card, and your address is printed or written on the envelope flap. "Do not use monogrammed cards for business correspondence," says a stationer.

"They are appropriate only for strictly social correspondence. The person you had dinner with shouldn't have to guess whose initials these are. A border is strictly for social cards, too, unless there is also a company logo."

Social sheet or half sheet. A half sheet can be used instead of a correspondence card and is an excellent choice for condolence notes. It folds over once and is inserted in an envelope. "A small, informal fold-over note, however, is only for social correspondence," according to one business stationery expert, "and it's generally not used by men."

Assorted small memo sheets are useful for cover notes to be sent along with reports and clippings. Many of them feature the user's name at the top or something like "From the desk of Nan Rosenthal." You can use them internally for "Great job!" notes to employees. Message cards bearing your name and title can also be attached to clippings and reports.

Business cards. For a business card, choose white or ecru stock with black or gray ink if you wish to convey a traditional image. You can write short messages on your business cards and clip them to articles or reports.

Stationery comes in many sizes and formats. It is available through retail stores and stationery catalogs in a wide range of prices and your individual style can be matched with good taste. For a little personal guidance, stop in at a good stationer's shop and ask to be educated about the different sizes, paper stocks, and style options available.

Paper Quality

When choosing your own stationery, you will want to consider the quality and practicality of the paper. Stationery is usually made of cotton fiber, wood pulp, or a combination of the two. Cotton fiber paper (known as rag paper) is appropriate for business, and most experts advise a minimum 25 percent cotton content for letterhead. For a truly impressive look, choose 100 percent cotton fiber paper.

The standard weight of good letterhead is 24 pounds. To get some idea of what this feels like, remember that copier paper is usually 20 pounds; memo sheets are usually 12 pounds. Some people prefer *very* heavy paper. If you are one of them, be sure to ask, "Can I put this through my laser printer?" Some laser printers can't accommodate very thick sheets. Use the same weight of stationery for the cover letter of a résumé as for the résumé itself. Invest in 100 percent cotton paper if you want your résumé to stand out.

The feel of the stock is a matter of personal choice. Some people like a very smooth paper; others prefer a texture. When choosing a business card, avoid coated stock, which is difficult to write on.

To Engrave or Not to Engrave

"I'm a traditionalist," says the owner of a small company, "so I always use engraved stationery when writing to an important customer or when I want to project a formal image. I have my business cards engraved, too. It's expensive, but your card is sometimes the only thing that people have to remind them of you."

For an elegant look, there's nothing like engraving, which produces sharp raised lettering. Because engraving uses a die, or copper plate, which you must buy, it's more expensive initially. But the die will last for many years, provided your address, phone, or fax number doesn't change.

The other options are printing and thermography, a process that creates a raised image, though a less distinctive one than engraving. Both of these methods are cheaper because there is no die charge.

In general, if you have to skimp somewhere, experts advise you to invest in good paper and use less expensive printing.

Alternatives

In some very casual situations you may want to use choices other than those already mentioned. Some people stay in touch by sending picture postcards, choosing a theme that relates to the recipient—such as a photo of Humphrey Bogart for someone who loves old movies. To thank a maître d' for a fine business lunch experience, an executive wrote on a blank greeting card illustrated with a still life of food.

You may also want to express your personality more freely on certain occasions when the recipient is a friend and image isn't an issue. The choice is a matter of judgment. Use yours.

Pens

Handwriting is more personal. It says, "I took the time to sit down and think about what I'm going to say." We love handwritten notes. We pay attention to them and we save them.

—*Executive vice president of a large advertising agency*

Think about it. A stack of mail sits on your desk and as you sift through, tossing some items into the trash and putting others aside to read later, you spot something hand-addressed in ink. Don't you often sit back and open it right away? There's something about handwriting that says, "Read me, read me," and people tend to respond.

Handwriting seems to add meaning to words, and the kind of pen you use can make a contribution and leave a good impression, too. "A thank-you note written on fine stock with a good fountain pen says you have class," according to a corporate consultant. "It implies that you are well-mannered, genteel, and thoughtful."

But there's more to pens than that. A good pen not only looks good on paper; it *feels* good in the hand. In a world of fast, efficient computers and busy schedules, where you jump from one project to the next, fine writing instruments are quietly luxurious. They have a timeless quality that seems to speak to the spirit—something you can't say about ninety-nine-cent ballpoints. If you're ready to move beyond disposables, here are some of your options.

Fountain Pens

Collectors rhapsodize about fine fountain pens, passionately describing the act of writing with them as a sensual experience. These pens seem to echo some lost refinement of the past.

"When you pick up a fountain pen and write to somebody, you want to reflect on what you're doing and take the time to really enjoy writing," says an authority on writing instruments. "Many things in life are more convenient, but are they more enjoyable? Writing with a quality pen is synonymous with great pleasure."

Once you notice the elegance of fountain-pen script, you'll appreciate the difference. A good pen allows you to be more expressive. "It's more fun to write with," says a fountain-pen fan, "because it gives a variety of thick and thin lines and a much smoother write. There's less strain on your fingers because you don't have to press down so hard. It's like using a paintbrush to layer ink on the page."

It's the nib that makes all the difference in fountain pens. The nib is the metal point that extends out of the pen and transmits ink to the page. High-quality pens have a pure gold nib with iridium at the tip. Iridium is a very strong platinum-based metal that will last a long time and give you a smooth line.

Fountain pens do have some drawbacks, however. They can be hard to use comfortably if you're unaccustomed to them, which may mean you need to practice.

Because you don't press down, you can't use a fountain pen to write on forms with carbon copies. That's why most fountain pen users own a roller ball pen as well.

Fountain pens can also be messy. Purists insist on filling them from an ink bottle, but you can buy fountain pens with disposable ink cartridges. Air travel can present a problem because the pressure during takeoff and landing can force the ink out, causing the pen to leak. The rule of thumb when flying, according to authorities, is to keep the pen either completely filled or completely empty to avoid trouble.

On the other hand, some people prefer fountain pens precisely because they slow you down and demand that you pay attention to them. They hark back to a bygone age when people had more free time. "We have computers that allow us to do tasks quicker, but we also have more tasks to do," says one expert. "When you write to somebody with a fountain pen, you can hone your writing skills and penmanship and take the time to really enjoy yourself."

Roller Ball Pens

Roller balls offer the advantages of a fountain pen and the convenience of a ballpoint. Many prefer them to fountain pens. "I write in longhand on 8½- by 11-inch white lined pads at work," says an accountant, "and I like a roller ball because it glides smoothly over the paper. It feels better than a fountain pen." For others who are intimidated by fountain pens, a roller ball can be an intermediate step.

A roller ball isn't messy, and it is refilled with cartridges. It writes on carbons, yet provides a smoother, more elegant line than a ballpoint. Its thin ink permits an easier flow than the viscous ink of a ballpoint. A roller ball also requires very little pressure, in contrast to a ballpoint, which you must press to get the ink out. Expect a roller ball refill to run out much more quickly, however, because the ink is water-based. In the past, roller balls had to be capped when not in use so that they wouldn't dry out. But the new capless models retract like some ballpoints and last much longer.

Ballpoint Pens

The ballpoint pen, designed as an alternative to the fountain pen, became popular in the late 1940s. These pens are less expensive than roller balls, and they last for many months. Ballpoints are practical and easy to use—some people have never tried anything else. But a note written in ballpoint lacks the polished look of a roller ball or fountain pen.

Buying a Pen

Shopping for a better pen can be as pleasurable an experience as writing with one. Making an informed purchase is a bit complicated, but it's fun to get educated. Ask yourself these questions as you set out to select the perfect pen for you:

How will you use the pen? Will you sign a check or write an address once in a while, or will you give the pen a heavy-duty daily workout? In the latter case, issues like weight are important. If you keep your pen in your pocket or purse most of the time, it doesn't matter how heavy it is.

How does it feel and write? Does the pen fit well in your hand? If you write for long periods of time, will it be comfortable? A pen should feel good, whether it's big, small, fat, or slim. A very thin pen can be hard on your hand if you use it for more than jotting down a few words now and then. "I don't like pens with ridges. I need one that's comfortable to use during a day of writing constantly," says one sales executive.

You want to choose a pen that suits your handwriting style. Does the ink flow quickly or slowly? Does the point provide a nice consistent line or a broken one? When buying a roller ball, the refill is also very important. You want a reliable one that will last and won't blot or skip.

Do you like a thick or thin line or something in-between—in other words, do you need a broad nib or a fine point? Try several pens out and write with them before you make up your mind.

Do you want a high-prestige pen? In a kind of reaction against technology, pens have become accessories. An elegant pen makes a statement. Like an expensive watch, a good pen is a status symbol. Is brand-name recognition important to you? Will you pull your pen out at board meetings? These are things to think about while making your choice.

How important is quality? If you care about the pen you choose, you want to be sure the company will be around next year for repairs and refills. When you take good care of a quality pen, it can last a century.

As one expert says, "You want a reputable dealer who will give you service, explain the history of the company, the materials, and the manufacturing process, and who can adjust the flow of ink to your liking and offer other advice. A specialist will know what to look for in your handwriting. If you have tiny hands, you don't want a very big pen; if you press very hard, you probably don't want a fine nib on a fountain pen. A flexible nib will give you both thick and thin lines. And if you're left-handed, there are special nibs for you."

How much do you want to spend? There's a perfect pen for everyone, and a good-quality pen can be affordable. Generally, the higher the price of the pen, the more handwork was involved in its manufacture; it will also be stronger and made of finer materials. In better ballpoints, for example, there's a difference in styling, materials, and design, though not always in the quality of the refills; a $60 pen may take the same refill as a far more expensive model.

Once you pass the $300 or so range in a fountain pen, you're paying for beauty, hand tooling, and materials like gold and platinum inlays. The price of a collectible vintage pen can go as high as six figures. Price depends on factors such as rarity of the model, the manufacturer, and the pen's condition. Certain pens from the early 1900s, for example, can fetch $10,000 or more. Limited-edition pens can also appreciate; some have doubled or tripled in value in a few years.

Do you hesitate to buy a good pen because you lose pens all the time? One expert says, "When I switched from ten-dollar sunglasses to expensive ones, I never lost another pair. You pay attention when you make an investment."

What's your style? There are so many companies making pens in so many styles that you can find something you'll enjoy, no matter what your taste or price range. There are retro looks and sleek modern pens, funky styles and classic ones. There are vintage models and the latest innovations, including ergonomic pens for people with arthritis or carpal tunnel syndrome. There is even a pen of the type used by astronauts, which allows you to write without interruption while lying on the couch or in bed. One advertising agency creative director gave these pens as inexpensive gifts at the office.

Choose a pen that will work for your life.

Reference Library

Dictionaries and other reference books are invaluable resources when you write notes and other types of correspondence. Here are some helpful basics for any library:

American Heritage Dictionary of the English Language, 3rd ed. Boston: Houghton Mifflin, 1992.

Bartlett, John. *Bartlett's Familiar Quotations,* 16th ed. Justin Kaplan, ed., Boston: Little, Brown, 1992.

Chapman, Robert, ed. *Roget's International Thesaurus,* 5th ed. New York: HarperCollins, 1992.

Feinberg, Steven L., ed. *Crane's Blue Book of Stationery.* New York: Doubleday, 1989.

Letitia Baldrige's New Complete Guide to Executive Manners. New York: Rawson Associates, 1993.

Magida, Arthur J. *How to Be a Perfect Stranger: A Guide to Etiquette in Other People's Religious Ceremonies.* Woodstock, Vt.: Jewish Lights Publishing, 1996.

Merriam Webster's Collegiate Dictionary, 10th ed. Springfield, Mass.: Merriam-Webster, 1993.

Pachter, Barbara, and Marjorie Brody, with Betsy Anderson. *Prentice Hall Complete Business Etiquette Handbook.* Englewood Cliffs, N.J.: Prentice Hall, 1995.

Strunk, William, Jr., and E. B. White. *The Elements of Style,* 3rd ed. New York: Macmillan, 1979.

Tripp, Rhoda Thomas, comp. *The International Thesaurus of Quotations.* New York: Harper & Row, 1970.